2018-2019 Edition

SAT Writing
New Grammar Tests

- Please visit PrepVantageTutoring.com for additional study materials and information regarding future book releases

ISBN-10: 1717239412; ISBN-13: 978-1717239419

SAT® is a registered trademark of the College Board, which does not endorse and is not affiliated with this product.

Visit us at **PrepVantageTutoring.com**

SAT Writing: New Grammar Tests, 2018-2019 Edition
Copyright © 2018 PrepVantage Publishing

ISBN-10: 1717239412; ISBN-13: 978-1717239419

Table of Contents

Test 1

Writing and Language

2018 SAT Practice

Writing and Language Test

35 MINUTES, 44 QUESTIONS

Turn to Section 2 of your answer sheet to answer the questions in this section.

DIRECTIONS

Each passage below is accompanied by a number of questions. For some questions, you will consider how the passage might be revised to improve the expression of ideas. For other questions, you will consider how the passage might be edited to correct errors in sentence structure, usage, or punctuation. A passage or a question may be accompanied by one or more graphics (such as a table or graph) that you will consider as you make revising and editing decisions.

Some questions will direct you to an underlined portion of a passage. Other questions will direct you to a location in a passage or ask you to think about the passage as a whole.

After reading each passage, choose the answer to each question that most effectively improves the quality of writing in the passage or that makes the passage conform to the conventions of standard written English. Many questions will include a "NO CHANGE" option. Choose that option if you think the best choice is to leave the relevant portion of the passage as it is.

Questions 1-11 are based on the following passage.

Is It Me, or Is This Interview Crowded?

A job interview is almost always a stressful experience, and many people worry that the other applicants being interviewed might be especially desirable. Imagine finding yourself in the same room as those individuals, being evaluated alongside one another. **1** In contrast, a group interview is a process in which

1

A) NO CHANGE
B) In addition,
C) For example,
D) By definition,

CONTINUE ➡

two or more job candidates are interviewed together by one or more hiring managers. It is important to understand the difference between a group interview **2** or a panel interview: in the latter case, only one candidate is **3** placed in respect at a time, but he or she is interviewed by more than one person. While a group interview might seem like a tense situation for an applicant, some employers find that this option is the best way to select the right candidate.

2
A) NO CHANGE
B) and
C) from
D) against

3
A) NO CHANGE
B) assessed
C) defined
D) hailed

CONTINUE

[4] Despite the benefits of group interviews, this new employment practice has met some resistance. In particular, if a job calls for someone who can work with others even if there are high stakes or competing opinions, interviewing applicants collectively can be a good way to simulate **[5]** anything that is there being re-created. Alternatively, if a group of candidates for designated roles **[6]** are intended to be hired at the same time (for example, retail employees hired for the holiday season, or interns who will work together for the summer), it may be logical to assess which candidates work most effectively together. **[7]** Simply choosing the most talented individuals may undermine the team dynamic. Some employers also simply find it more efficient to interview in a group format rather than going through the lengthy process of holding many individual interviews.

4

Which choice most effectively introduces the discussion that follows?

A) NO CHANGE

B) The popularity of group interviews has been documented by human resources departments.

C) A few of the standard arguments against group interviews are fundamentally unsound.

D) Group interviews are typically used to screen candidates for roles that demand collaboration.

5

A) NO CHANGE

B) what things they are being asked about.

C) those conditions.

D) them.

6

A) NO CHANGE

B) are being

C) being

D) is

7

The writer is considering deleting the underlined portion. Should this content be kept or deleted?

A) Kept, because it provides a logical reason for utilizing group interviews.

B) Kept, because it calls attention to the likely outcome of a group interview.

C) Deleted, because it contradicts the writer's thesis.

D) Deleted, because it repeats earlier content.

CONTINUE

[1] The nature of a group interview means that candidates need to be strategic and cooperative if they want to succeed. [2] It is very important to show a positive and friendly attitude towards other applicants and to not behave in an aggressive or **8** overt competitive manner. [3] If the candidates are asked to work together to complete a task, individuals should be supportive of each other's ideas and suggestions. [4] For example, if all of the applicants are asked to respond to the same question, **9** they're important to make sure that an answer contributes something new and doesn't simply echo what others have said. [5] During a group activity, showing leadership by suggesting compromises between different opinions **10** or asking guiding questions to direct a conversation can also be very impressive. [6] At the same time, each applicant still needs to find ways to stand out and attract the attention of the hiring managers. **11**

8

A) NO CHANGE
B) competitive, overtly
C) overtly competitive
D) competitively to overt

9

A) NO CHANGE
B) there's
C) it's
D) its'

10

A) NO CHANGE
B) or to ask guiding
C) or to ask to guide
D) or being asked as guiding

11

For the sake of logic and coherence, sentence 6 should be placed
A) where it is now.
B) after sentence 1.
C) after sentence 2.
D) after sentence 3.

CONTINUE

Test 1

Questions 12-22 are based on the following passage.

The Legacy of Martha Graham

Dance aficionados recognize Martha Graham as one of the greatest artists of the 20th century. Her style of contemporary dance is considered both inventive and timeless. Born in 1884 in the Pittsburgh, Pennsylvania area, [12] the establishment of Graham's first school of dance took place in 1926 in New York City.

Graham's innovative methods grew from her experimentation with the body's physical movements of contraction and release. The sharp yet graceful and natural style that defined her dance technique was a departure from the types that were [13] currently being taught and performed at the time. Graham's creativity traversed artistic boundaries. She embraced a multitude of [14] genres: including the visual arts, fashion, and music. Her style has influenced the generation of famous dancers and choreographers that includes Merce Cunningham, Paul Taylor, and Twyla Tharp. [15] The synthesis of styles and inspirations that Graham achieved was, indeed, astonishing when it first appeared.

12

A) NO CHANGE

B) New York City was where Graham established her first school of dance in 1926.

C) Graham established her first school of dance in 1926 in New York City.

D) Graham's first school of dance was established in 1926 in New York City.

13

A) NO CHANGE

B) being taught, performed, and put into action at the time.

C) being taught by instructors and performed at the time.

D) being taught and performed at the time.

14

A) NO CHANGE

B) genres including:

C) genres, including

D) genres including,

15

Which choice most effectively indicates that Graham's ideas continue to be influential?

A) NO CHANGE

B) Today, the Martha Graham Dance School is a leading force in the world of dance.

C) Of these individuals, only Cunningham would approach Graham's status as a dance celebrity.

D) Even now, her ideas remain a source of interest among scholars of modern dance.

CONTINUE

The Martha Graham School is located in the West Village of New York City. It is the oldest professional school of dance in the United States, with the focus of the curriculum placed [16] mainly of the Martha Graham Technique and repertory. The faculty consists of current and former members of the Martha Graham Dance Company, some of [17] them actually trained with Graham.

Since its beginnings, the Martha Graham Dance Company has been renowned throughout the world and has performed in more than 50 countries, [18] on continents ranging from South America to Asia. Moreover, 85% of the members of the Company have trained at the Martha Graham School.

16

A) NO CHANGE
B) mainly on
C) mainly to
D) mainly with

17

A) NO CHANGE
B) whom
C) that
D) these members

18

The writer is considering deleting the underlined portion and concluding the sentence with a period after "countries." Should the underlined content be kept or deleted?

A) Kept, because it helps to clarify the scope of the Martha Graham Dance Company.

B) Kept, because it explains why the Martha Graham Dance Company has become popular.

C) Deleted, because it contradicts the writer's argument that the Martha Graham Dance Company is a centralized organization.

D) Deleted, because it detracts from the passage's main focus on Martha Graham's influence on artists based in New York.

CONTINUE

[1] One of Graham's most famous works is *Appalachian Spring*, which originally premiered in 1944 on The Library of Congress stage. [2] With music by Aaron Copeland, the piece is performed by a troupe of male and female dancers. [3] Graham's central narrative tells of a spring celebration of American pioneers in the 19th century who have just built a farmhouse on their land. [4] The main characters are a bride, a groom, a pioneer woman, and a preacher. [5] The piece **19** <u>exaggerates</u> the rugged optimism of the characters and conveys a sense of joy, **20** <u>even when</u> Graham's narrative turns to the struggles of pioneer life. [6] When *Appalachian Spring* first premiered, Graham herself danced the lead role of the bride. **21**

19

A) NO CHANGE
B) accentuates
C) personifies
D) hypothesizes

20

A) NO CHANGE
B) even where
C) and
D) DELETE the underlined portion.

21

The writer wishes to insert the following sentence

> During her career, Graham created 181 masterpiece dance compositions, many of which are still regularly performed.

The most logical and appropriate placement for this sentence would be

A) before sentence 1.
B) before sentence 2.
C) after sentence 5.
D) after sentence 6.

CONTINUE

Describing dancers and artists, Martha Graham once said, "You are unique, and if that is not fulfilled, then something has been lost." Graham died in 1991 at the age of 96. Her eminent **22** and, in its own way truly unique career elevated dance as an art form. She both trained and inspired generations of dancers, and left a legacy that will long be celebrated.

A) NO CHANGE

B) and in its own way, truly

C) and, in its own way, truly

D) and, in its own way truly,

CONTINUE

Questions 23-33 are based on the following passage.

Bike-Sharing Choices: To Dock, or Not to Dock?

In the past fifteen years, participation in the [23] "sharing economy"—a term that encompasses pay-per-use practices in transportation, travel, and access to goods—has grown considerably. Perhaps one of the most triumphant narratives in the current sharing economy is the story of bike-sharing programs. Easy to use and friendly to the environment, the form of bike-sharing that has appeared in major United States cities involves strategically [24] located terminals. Each of these terminals is stocked with multiple bikes. A swipe of a credit card can unlock a single bike for a set period; it is up to a given bike's temporary user to return [25] the bikes' on time and undamaged. However, the absence of any other obligations makes bike-sharing efficient, case-specific, and in some cases cheaper than owning a bike.

23

A) NO CHANGE

B) "sharing economy," a term—that encompasses pay-per-use practices

C) "sharing economy," a term that encompasses—pay-per-use practices

D) "sharing economy" a term that encompasses pay-per-use practices—

24

Which choice best combines the sentences at the underlined portion?

A) located terminals, each one

B) located terminals; each of them

C) located terminals, and each of those ones is

D) located terminals: each, being

25

A) NO CHANGE

B) the bikes on time

C) the bike's on time

D) the bike on time

CONTINUE

Bike-sharing [26] has got itself going today in cities worldwide. Some bike-sharing programs are notable for their rapid growth: [27] Manhattan's version of bike-sharing, Citi Bike, because it first appeared in 2013 grew to 12,000 bikes by 2018. Others (such as Hangzhou's 70,000-bike program) are notable for their seeming omni-presence, while still others (such as Montreal's adored, 5200-bike Bixi Bike fleet) [28] continue to face marketing obstacles that can be overcome with time and patience.

26

A) NO CHANGE
B) is to the positive
C) thrives
D) awes

27

Which of the following is the most logical version of the underlined portion?

A) NO CHANGE
B) Manhattan's version of bike-sharing, because it was Citi Bike, first appeared in 2013, growing
C) Manhattan's version of bike-sharing, Citi Bike, first appeared in 2013 and grew
D) Manhattan's version of bike-sharing, because it was Citi Bike, although first appearing in 2013 soon grew

---

28

Which choice best supports both the writer's characterization of Bixi Bike and the main ideas presented in this paragraph?

A) NO CHANGE
B) offer higher quality service to compensate for a smaller fleet.
C) generate intense customer loyalty with relatively few vehicles.
D) are determined to emulate the fast-paced growth of Citi Bike.

CONTINUE

Nonetheless, there is one trait that almost all of the most successful bike-sharing programs have in common. Each one uses mass-produced bikes that are set up at docking stations. [29] While the obligation to pay using a major credit card may be a nuisance to some riders, there is evidence that bike-sharing based on different premises—including greater flexibility in terms of drop-off— [30] araised considerable liabilities.

Dock-less bike-sharing is an alternative method that some cities in China have adopted. Under this approach, bikes are equipped with specialized locks that can be opened through a digital payment. It is then the responsibility of the bike's user, once the paid-for usage time has concluded, [31] re-locking the bike at an appropriate location. Unfortunately, this system raises the possibility that an irresponsible user will lock the bike at an inappropriate location, perhaps in the middle of a busy sidewalk or on private property.

29

The writer wishes to describe a problem unique to a dock-based bike-sharing format. Which choice best accomplishes this goal?

A) NO CHANGE

B) While the possibility of being charged for damage to a rented bike

C) While being required to "report" to one of a handful of locations

D) While the inability to customize a "sharing economy" vehicle

30

A) NO CHANGE

B) rose

C) raise

D) raises

31

A) NO CHANGE

B) to re-lock

C) as re-locking

D) having to re-lock

CONTINUE

There is another potential problem with dock-less bike-sharing: vandalism. In Beijing and other Chinese metropolises, residents have bent, broken, and even burned sharing economy bikes. Such violent responses can be difficult to prevent or [32] (should they occur) penalize when the bikes are more difficult to monitor, as is naturally the case in a de-centralized bike-sharing system. Cities such as New York—which has experimented with dock-less bike sharing but has never instituted a dock-less system comparable to Citi Bike—are rightly wary of the approach that [33] will have caused such problems in Beijing. For now, docking stations are a necessary element of the future of bike-sharing.

32

The writer wishes to revise the underlined portion to read as follows.

(should they occur in a fashion that may cause measurable damage)

Should the writer make this revision?

A) Yes, because it helps the reader to understand that damage to sharing economy bikes can in fact be prevented.

B) Yes, because it more fully explains a specific flaw of the bike-sharing systems in Chinese cities.

C) No, because it wrongly introduces a tone of uncertainty into a discussion of an unavoidable problem.

D) No, because it does not add further specifics to the discussion of violent responses to sharing economy bikes.

33

A) NO CHANGE

B) will cause

C) would cause

D) has caused

CONTINUE

Test 1

Questions 34-44 are based on the following passage and supplementary material.

Understanding a Star's Life Cycle

Stars burn for billions of years, and so the birth, evolution, and death of a star are significant events. The stages of a star's life cycle, each drastically different from the others, are nebula, star, red giant, red dwarf, white dwarf, supernova, neutron star, and black hole. Astronomers have observed many fascinating **34** properties of stars, but, we still have more to learn about these incredible celestial bodies.

A nebula is a large cloud of interstellar dust that will coalesce into a star. After a star **35** burns through its hydrogen, it expands drastically into a red giant, which is 10 to 1,000 times as wide as the Sun. The red giant eventually loses mass and volume, collapsing into a red dwarf (only one tenth as wide as our Sun). The red dwarf then morphs into a white dwarf. Despite being very hot, white dwarfs are only roughly **36** 10% as bright as the Sun, to take the accepted maximum. The white dwarf eventually explodes into a supernova, which is briefly ~100 billion times as bright as the Sun.

34

A) NO CHANGE

B) properties of stars; but, we

C) properties of stars, however, we

D) properties of stars; however, we

35

A) NO CHANGE

B) gets done with

C) spends down

D) wastes

36

The writer wishes to include accurate information from the following tables.

Width Compared to Sun (Factor)

Type	Minimum	Maximum
Red Giant	10	1000
White Dwarf	0.1	0.5

Brightness Compared to Sun (Factor)

Type	Minimum	Maximum
Red Giant	0.5	0.75
White Dwarf	0.001	0.01

Which choice accomplishes this goal?

A) NO CHANGE

B) 10% less bright than the Sun, to take the accepted maximum.

C) 1% as bright as the Sun, to take the accepted maximum.

D) 1% less bright than the Sun, to take the accepted maximum.

CONTINUE

Supernovae from particularly heavy stars leave behind extremely dense neutron stars. Neutron stars [37] are named it when the explosion of their predecessor supernovae forces protons and electrons to combine into neutrons. If the remnants of a supernova are heavy enough, they will instead implode into a black hole, which is even denser than a neutron star.

[1] Astronomers often report masses, starting with those of objects in our solar system, in terms of solar mass (M$\odot$). [2] So, for example, a star weighing 8×10^{30} kg would be listed as [38] a mass of 4 M$\odot$. [3] One M$\odot$ is equal to the mass of [39] their Sun (approximately 2×10^{30} kg). [4] The Chandrasekhar limit, the maximum mass of a white dwarf star before it becomes unstable, is also measured in M$\odot$: it is approximately 1.4 M$\odot$. [5] However, limits are apparently not absolute. [40]

37

A) NO CHANGE
B) are so named because
C) are named like they are since
D) are named that, where

38

A) NO CHANGE
B) though a mass
C) being a mass
D) having a mass

39

A) NO CHANGE
B) its
C) one's
D) our

40

To make the order of ideas in the paragraph most logical, sentence 3 should be placed

A) where it is now.
B) after sentence 1.
C) after sentence 4.
D) after sentence 5.

CONTINUE

[41] The Supernova Legacy Survey was a project that monitored over 2,000 supernovae for five consecutive years. In 2003, the survey observed the SNLS-03D3bb supernova, which was later named the Champagne Supernova. Many astronomers believe that the Champagne Supernova was generated from a white dwarf that [42] has twice the Sun's mass. Thus, its mass was approximately 2 M⊙, well beyond the Chandrasekhar limit.

Based on the graph, which choice provides the most relevant and accurate description of the Supernova Legacy Project?

A) NO CHANGE

B) The Supernova Legacy Survey was a project that monitored almost 2,000 supernovae in each of the last four years.

C) The Supernova Legacy Survey was designed to monitor a variety of celestial events, but eventually came to focus almost entirely on supernovae.

D) The Supernova Legacy Survey discovered an increasing number of supernovae in the universe from 2014 to 2015.

42

A) NO CHANGE

B) had

C) is

D) will be

Elements of the Universe Studied by the Supernova Legacy Survey

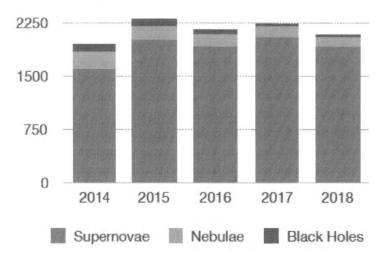

CONTINUE

How did this white dwarf manage to exceed the Chandrasekhar limit? It may have done so by spinning particularly quickly, which would have given it extra structural stability, or [43] it may have been formed by two white dwarfs combining into one star before exploding. Professional astronomers continue to study the skies in the hope [44] discovered more about these celestial events.

43

Which choice most effectively presents a new and detailed response to the question that begins the paragraph?

A) NO CHANGE

B) it may have reached a mass that is twice that of the sun through a very different means of transformation.

C) it may have surpassed the Chandrasekhar limit by some other method that resulted in physical changes.

D) it may have been created by an especially rapid rotational movement.

44

A) NO CHANGE

B) discovering

C) of discovering

D) for discovering

STOP
**If you finish before time is called, you may check your work on this section only.
Do not turn to any other section.**

Answer Key: Test 1

Passage 1		Passage 2		Passage 3		Passage 4	
1.	D	12.	C	23.	A	34.	D
2.	B	13.	D	24.	A	35.	A
3.	B	14.	C	25.	D	36.	C
4.	D	15.	B	26.	C	37.	B
5.	C	16.	B	27.	C	38.	D
6.	D	17.	B	28.	C	39.	D
7.	A	18.	A	29.	C	40.	B
8.	C	19.	B	30.	D	41.	B
9.	C	20.	A	31.	B	42.	B
10.	A	21.	A	32.	D	43.	A
11.	D	22.	C	33.	D	44.	C

Topic Areas by Question

Expression of Ideas

Passage 1: Questions 1, 3-5, 7, 11

Passage 2: Questions 13, 15, 18-21

Passage 3, Questions 24, 26-29, 32

Passage 4, Questions 35-37, 40-41, 43

Standard English Conventions

Passage 1: Questions 2, 6, 8-10

Passage 2: Questions 12, 14, 16-17, 22

Passage 3, Questions 23, 25, 30-31, 33

Passage 4, Questions 34, 38-39, 42, 44

Answer Explanations
Test 1, Pages 2-17

Passage 1, Pages 2-5

1. D is the correct answer.

The sentence that contains the underlined portion explains that a group interview "is a process" and thus provides a definition. Choose D and eliminate A, since the writer is providing related facts about group interviews rather than establishing clearly contrasting ideas. Eliminate B and C: the transition needs to clarify a general term ("group interview") from the preceding content, but does not add events or examples to the specific scenario ("Imagine finding . . .") mentioned earlier.

2. B is the correct answer.

In standard English usage, "between . . . and" is the accepted pairing for listing two items regardless of circumstance. Choose B and eliminate A (which wrongly indicates alternatives, not a list), as well as C and D (which indicate difference or opposition).

3. B is the correct answer.

The underlined word should describe what happens to a "candidate" during a group interview. Such a candidate would be evaluated or "assessed" in terms of job skills and suitability. Choose B and eliminate A (which involves movement), C (which involves concepts or portrayal), and D (which indicates greeting) as introducing the wrong contexts for an interview evaluation.

4. D is the correct answer.

The paragraph describes "a good way" and a "logical" use for group interviews, so that D rightly refers to how group interviews are suitable for screening purposes (especially for roles that involve group or collaboration skills). Eliminate A and C as answers that wrongly indicate possible negatives, since the paragraph is thoroughly positive about group interviews. B wrongly mentions "human resources departments," which are not directly described anywhere in the paragraph.

5. C is the correct answer.

This question requires concise yet specific phrasing that describes the workplace events, situations, or "conditions" that a group interview simulates. Choose C and eliminate A and B as needlessly wordy. D involves an ambiguous pronoun (since "them" could refer to "stakes," "opinions," or "applicants") and should this be eliminated.

6. D is the correct answer.

The subject of the underlined verb is "group," which is singular. Choose D and eliminate A and B (which are both plural). C creates a sentence fragment and should be eliminated for this reason.

7. A is the correct answer.

The underlined portion explains how hiring based on group considerations (rather than individual talent) can create a "team dynamic." Choose A since the writer indicates a reason for using group interviews INSTEAD of another method. B wrongly indicates that the sentence is about a group interview's OUTCOME (not the indicated PREMISE of a group interview) and thus considers the wrong factor. Keep in mind that the sentence supports the writer's positive stance about group interviews (eliminating C) and offers a new thought about "talented individuals" (not a thought mentioned earlier, eliminating D).

8. C is the correct answer.

The word "manner" should be modified by an adjective, which can itself be modified by an adverb. C, "overtly competitive," offers a construction of this sort. A wrongly modifies the adjective "competitive" with another adjective, while B and D both wrongly modify the noun "manner" with an adverb.

9. C is the correct answer.

For setting out a recommendation, as in the sentence that contains the underlined portion, the contraction "it's" (as in "it's a good idea") is an appropriate choice. Choose C and eliminate A (a non-standard usage that also wrongly indicates that "they" [the applicants] are "important"). B is better suited to describing a place, while D is a nonexistent form.

10. A is the correct answer.

The word "asking" is in parallel with "suggesting," so that A is an appropriate choice. Eliminate B and C, since both answers break the parallelism with "to guide," while D is needlessly wordy and also illogically indicates that an applicant would be similar to ("as") a question.

11. <u>D</u> is the correct answer.

Sentence 6 calls attention to the need to "stand out" in an interview, while sentence 4 provides an "example" of how an applicant can stand out through his or her answers. Choose D and eliminate A (since sentence 6 ALSO provides a transition away from the theme of collaboration in sentence 3). B and C would both wrongly break up the early discussion of collaboration-based skills with content about how an individual candidate can stand out.

Passage 2, Pages 6-9

12. <u>C</u> is the correct answer.

When a sentence consists of the structure [introductory phrase —> comma —> independent clause], the introductory phrase must modify the first noun after the comma. Thus, the first noun after the comma must be a person based on the introductory phrase ("Born in 1884 . . . "). Choice C is the only choice in which the first noun is a person. Note that D starts with "Graham's first school" so the noun is school ("Graham's" is a possessive adjective, NOT a noun).

13. <u>D</u> is the correct answer.

When you see answer choices that are subsets of other choices, check for redundancy within the answer choice and with the rest of the paragraph. D isn't redundant, so it is correct. A is redundant due to "currently" and "at the time," B is redundant due to "performed" and "put into action," and C is redundant due to "taught" and "by instructors."

14. <u>C</u> is the correct answer.

The choices for this question differ only in their punctuation, so this is a punctuation question. The phrase that starts with "including" should be separated by a comma from the independent clause. Thus, C is correct. D puts the comma in the wrong place, while A and B incorrectly use a colon (although the colon would be correct if "including" weren't present).

15. <u>B</u> is the correct answer.

The goal in this question is to indicate that Graham's ideas are STILL INFLUENTIAL. B is right because it shows the lasting influence of Graham's dance school. A is about the past, C is about Cunningham, and D says that scholars find Graham's work interesting (not influential).

16. <u>B</u> is the correct answer.

The correct phrasing with "focus" is to "focus ON" something. Thus, B is correct. "Focus of/to/with" are not correct standard idiom phrases, so A, C, and D are wrong. It helps to notice that "of the curriculum" is a prepositional phrase and thus the sentence can be read without it.

17. <u>B</u> is the correct answer.

The correct object pronoun for people is "whom," when the word "people" designates the object of a sentence. Thus, B is correct. C is wrong because "that" is for a thing, not people. Commas cannot join two sentences; only semicolons can. Thus, A and D are wrong.

18. <u>A</u> is the correct answer.

The underlined portion gives examples of the continents on which the dance company has performed. If deleted, the reader would still know that the company has performed in more than 50 countries but not how far apart those countries are. Thus, A is correct. B is wrong because the underlined portion doesn't state a reason, while C and D are wrong because they contain incorrect statements about the passage's focus.

19. <u>B</u> is the correct answer.

This is a word choice question, so it is helpful to come up with your own word to substitute for the underlined word. The meaning there is "highlights" so B is the best match. A is negative and unsupported, while C and D are off-topic.

20. <u>A</u> is the correct answer.

This sentence talks about a time in the narrative, so "when" (choice A) is an appropriate word to use. Joy and struggles are contrasting ideas, so "and" (choice C) doesn't work as a connector, while "even" does work. B is wrong because "where" is for locations. D would create a comma splice.

21. <u>C</u> is the correct answer.

The indented sentence discusses Graham's 181 masterpieces, while sentence 1 talks about one of those pieces. Thus, the indented sentence is a topic sentence and should go before sentence 1, so Choice A is correct. Choices B, C, and D are wrong because the general statement should precede the specific example rather than follow it. Additionally, B and C are wrong because they interrupt the discussion of *Appalachian Spring* with a sentence that is not about *Appalachian Spring*.

22. <u>C</u> is the correct answer.

The choices for this question differ only in their punctuation, so this is a punctuation question. The phrase "in its own way" should be separated by a pair of commas from the rest of the sentence. Thus, C is correct, while

A and B are each missing one of the commas. D puts the comma in the wrong place by separating "truly" from the word that it modifies, "unique."

Passage 3, Pages 10-13

23. A is the correct answer.

Phrases that can be set off with a pair of commas may also be set off with a pair of dashes. Such a phrase should be non-essential to the sentence so that, when it is deleted, the remainder is still a sentence. Choice A is correct because the phrase between the two dashes in the sentence can be deleted and the sentence still makes sense, while the remainder doesn't make sense in B or C. With D, the remainder is a sentence but it incorrectly divides "practices in" with a dash and is missing a punctuation mark after "sharing economy."

24. A is the correct answer.

The two sentences are wordy due to the repetition of "terminals." To be more concise, "each one" in choice A should be used. B is wrong because a semicolon requires an independent clause on either side or a list with commas in the items. C is wrong because "those ones" is redundant. D is wrong because of the incorrect use of "being" and because a comma should not split a subject from its verb.

25. D is the correct answer.

"A given bike" is a singular noun so D is correct. A and B are plural, so they are wrong. C is incorrectly possessive because "the bike's" isn't immediately followed by a noun (e.g. "the bike's handlebars").

26. C is the correct answer.

This is a word choice question, so it is helpful to come up with your own word to substitute for the underlined word. The meaning here is "does well," so C is the best match. A and B are too informal. D is wrong because is ascribes a human trait to a non-living phenomenon.

27. C is the correct answer.

The sentence states that Manhattan's first bike sharing program was Citi Bike, which grew between 2013 and 2018. There is no reason or cause and effect stated, so there is no need for the word "because." Thus, C is right, while A, B, and D incorrectly use the word "because."

28. C is the correct answer.

The goal in this question is to support the main ideas of the paragraph (number of bikes per company) and the notion that Bixi Bike is "adored." C is right because "intense customer loyalty" matches "adored" and "relatively few vehicles" is about the number of bikes. A is negative, which contradicts the paragraph's topic sentence. D is unsupported, while the second part of B is relevant but the first part is not.

29. C is the correct answer.

The goal in this question is to present a problem unique to dock-based bike-sharing. C is right because it presents a problem inherent in using docks. A, B, and D present problems that can be present with dock-less bike-sharing too, so that they do not fulfill the goal.

30. D is the correct answer.

This is a verb question. The sentence is in present tense (as shown by other verbs, such as "is"), and the subject (bike-sharing) is singular. Thus, D is right. Choice A isn't a word, B is past tense, and C is plural.

31. B is the correct answer.

It helps to read the sentence without the phrase sectioned off by commas ("once the paid-for usage time has concluded"). Thus, we have: "It is then the responsibility of the bike's user ___" so the next word should be "to." Thus, B must be right because it fits the standard idiomatic phrase "responsibility to." A omits a preposition entirely, while C and D both present non-standard transitions and break the idiom.

32. D is the correct answer.

The topic sentence of this paragraph is about vandalism to shared bikes, and the next sentence list types of bike damage. Thus, the longer parenthetical phrase in this question is redundant and should not be added, so eliminate A and B. Choice D is right because not adding further specifics aligns with being redundant. C is wrong because the parenthetical isn't uncertain and because the reason stated in choice C isn't related to redundancy.

33. D is the correct answer.

This is a verb question. The sentence is in present tense (as shown by other verbs, such as "are"). Thus, D is right. Choices A and B are future (regular future and future perfect) tenses, and C is subjunctive.

Passage 4, Pages 14-17

34. D is the correct answer.

In standard usage, a sentence may start with "However" but not with "But." Thus, the wording of A and B doesn't form two sentences, while the wording in C and D does. So, D is correct in that a semicolon separates two independent clauses. Eliminate B and C (a semicolon must separate two independent clauses; a comma cannot be used instead). A is wrong because "but" isn't an aside, which you can tell because it isn't removable from the sentence.

35. <u>A</u> is the correct answer.

Stars "burn through" fuel as they put it to use, just as machines do. Thus, A is correct. B and C feature informal or awkward wording, while D is inappropriately negative.

36. <u>C</u> is the correct answer.

Since the issue is white dwarf brightness, look at the second row of the second table. The maximum is 0.01, which is 1%. So, C is correct. D is wrong because 1% less would be 99% of the Sun's brightness (0.99 as a decimal).

37. <u>B</u> is the correct answer.

B correctly fixes the wording of the sentence. "When" is used for time and "where" is used for location. Neither applies here, so that A and D are wrong. C is unnecessarily wordy.

38. <u>D</u> is the correct answer.

Stars HAVE mass; they aren't mass. Thus, D is right and A and B (which create a faulty comparison between a star and a mass) are wrong. C is wrong because "as though a mass" would need to be followed by a verb.

39. <u>D</u> is the correct answer.

The Sun belongs to us, as indicated by the earlier reference to "our solar system," so the correct possessive pronoun is "our" in choice D. A, B, and C are wrong because the Sun doesn't belong to them/it/someone, all pronoun references that are undefined or ambiguous in context.

40. <u>B</u> is the correct answer.

Sentence 3 defines a solar mass unit. Terms should be defined before they are otherwise used, so this sentence needs to go before sentence 2. Thus, B is right. The other three choices have the definition of solar mass occurring after sentence 2, and thus disrupt a discussion that REQUIRES a clear definition of solar mass.

41. <u>B</u> is the correct answer.

Choice B is right because the graph shows a supernova (dark gray) bar of roughly 2,000 for five years (2014-2018), so that the four-year requirement in this answer is met. Choice A is wrong because fewer than 2000 supernovae were monitored in 2014, while choice C is wrong because the graph doesn't show the purpose of the survey, only its results. Choice D is wrong because the graph shows what was studied, NOT what was discovered (as attention to the graph title reveals).

42. <u>B</u> is the correct answer.

This is a verb question. The sentence is in past tense (as shown by "was generated") and describes possible completed events in the formation of a supernova. Thus, B is right. Choices A and C are present tense, and D is future tense. Even though "believe" is present tense, scientific theories are stated in present tense even if they involve past events, so that does not change the sentence tense to present.

43. <u>A</u> is the correct answer.

The goal in this question is to present NEW and DETAILED information. A is right because it presents specific, non-redundant information. B and C are vague and D is redundant with the first part of the sentence, so that these answers do not fulfill the goal.

44. <u>C</u> is the correct answer.

The correct phrasing is "in the hope OF _____ing" so C is right. B is missing the preposition. D uses the wrong preposition ("for" instead of "of"). A is missing the preposition and uses the wrong verb tense.

Test 2

Writing and Language

2018 SAT Practice

Test 2

Writing and Language Test

35 MINUTES, 44 QUESTIONS

Turn to Section 2 of your answer sheet to answer the questions in this section.

DIRECTIONS

Each passage below is accompanied by a number of questions. For some questions, you will consider how the passage might be revised to improve the expression of ideas. For other questions, you will consider how the passage might be edited to correct errors in sentence structure, usage, or punctuation. A passage or a question may be accompanied by one or more graphics (such as a table or graph) that you will consider as you make revising and editing decisions.

Some questions will direct you to an underlined portion of a passage. Other questions will direct you to a location in a passage or ask you to think about the passage as a whole.

After reading each passage, choose the answer to each question that most effectively improves the quality of writing in the passage or that makes the passage conform to the conventions of standard written English. Many questions will include a "NO CHANGE" option. Choose that option if you think the best choice is to leave the relevant portion of the passage as it is.

Questions 1-11 are based on the following passage and supplementary material.

Birdwatching with a Purpose

Many people regard birdwatching as a leisurely hobby, one that is dominated by older people. [1] The truth, however, is much more complex. Modern birdwatching is linked to the National Audubon Society, a non-profit conservation organization that is focused on birds. The Society works throughout the

---

1

Which choice most effectively introduces the discussion that follows?

A) NO CHANGE

B) In reality, the elderly have little involvement in modern birdwatching.

C) Birdwatchers themselves find such a conception ridiculous.

D) Though prevalent, this idea is absolutely absurd.

Americas using science, advocacy, education, and sophisticated conservation tactics. Among its many successes, the Society has aided in the restoration of the Florida Everglades and the Long Island Sound, as well as in protecting fragile habitats that include the Arctic National Wildlife Refuge. Society officials **2** accumulate nearly 500 chapters nationwide, all with members who engage in grassroots action.

A large number of individuals is involved with the National Audubon Society as "citizen scientists," who are notable for **3** forming an ethical aggregation during the organization's annual Christmas Bird Count and the Coastal Bird Survey. The Society **4** maintains a total of 23 state programs, also 41 nature centers, and there are nearly 500 local chapters that all work together.

The Audubon Christmas Bird Count is the longest running community science bird project. People of all ages participate in the event. The Christmas Bird Count has become an important source of information **5** for researchers: studying the ongoing status and ranges of bird populations across the Americas.

2
A) NO CHANGE
B) supervise
C) pursue
D) scan

3
A) NO CHANGE
B) collecting visual data
C) getting near to the truth
D) making the facts real

4
A) NO CHANGE
B) maintains a total of 23 state programs and 41 nature centers, and also nearly
C) maintains a total of 23 state programs, 41 nature centers, and nearly
D) maintains a total of 23 state programs, 41 nature centers, nearly

5
A) NO CHANGE
B) for: researchers studying
C) for researchers studying:
D) for researchers studying

CONTINUE

Perhaps one of the most alluring elements of birdwatching is that it can be pursued any time or anywhere. According to statistics corroborated by a 2016 national survey of Fishing, Hunting, and Wildlife-Associated Recreation that was produced by the U.S. Fish & Wildlife Service, **6** roughly 45 million birdwatching excursions, either near home or away from home, were placed on record.

As people become more interested in birdwatching, **7** it tends to invest in tourism, travel, and equipment in order to view and identify more species. Trips to wildlife reserves, national parks, coastal regions, and mountainous areas provide people with more opportunities to see rare birds in natural habitats. As a recreational practice, birdwatching, along with other forms of wildlife watching, contributes billions of **8** dollars of the United States economy.

Birdwatchers (by Million per Year) in the U.S.

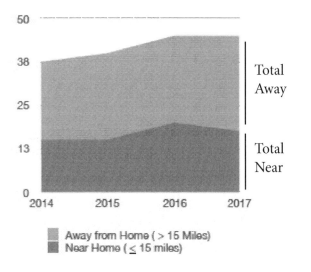

6

Which choice offers an accurate interpretation of the graph as the source of the "statistics" mentioned in the sentence?

A) NO CHANGE

B) there are roughly 45 million people who watch birds either around their homes or away from home.

C) birdwatching away from home is becoming as popular as birdwatching near home.

D) birdwatching, whether near home or away from home, will continue to grow in popularity.

7

A) NO CHANGE

B) one tends

C) he or she tends

D) they tend

8

A) NO CHANGE

B) dollars to

C) dollars from

D) dollars by

CONTINUE

An excellent example of how birding influences an economy is evident in a 2011 study by Texas A&M University. The University concluded that nature tourism, dominated by people who watch birds, brings over $300 million a year to the economy of the Rio Grand Valley in Texas. [9] Located at the southernmost tip of South Texas, the Rio Grand Valley features scenic tourist destinations that include Laguna Atascosa National Wildlife Refuge and the Santa Ana National Wildlife Refuge, [10] both are prime spots for avid birdwatchers.

[11] Although individuals put out backyard feeders to attract local bird species, engage with organizations like the National Audubon Society, or travel to exotic locations to view rare birds, these Americans have found intriguing ways to participate in modern birdwatching.

9

The writer wishes to insert a sentence that effectively transitions between topics. Which choice best achieves this goal?

A) Some birdwatchers may never know the extent of this financial benefit.

B) Though notable, such numbers do not capture the full role of birdwatching in revitalizing the area.

C) In its own right, the area offers its visitors an alluring natural landscape.

D) Ironically, birdwatching is seldom motivated by financial considerations.

10

A) NO CHANGE

B) both prime spots

C) each are prime spots

D) each prime spots

11

A) NO CHANGE

B) Whereas

C) Until

D) Whether

CONTINUE

Test 2

Food Writing for Thought

Whenever people dine out, they can share their opinions about a restaurant on web sites like Yelp and TripAdvisor. Reviews are easy to write and are posted along with a 1- to 5-point rating. These reviews can vary widely depending on individual **12** experience as are often very subjective. While people in cities such as New York are cautious about consulting sites like Yelp before dining out, **13** readers trust well more than half of today's professional food writers as sources of accurate information about a restaurant.

12

A) NO CHANGE

B) experience but are often

C) experience and are often

D) experience, often which are

13

Which choice presents the most accurate and relevant information from the two charts given below?

A) NO CHANGE

B) readers are only skeptical of a small minority of professional food writers

C) readers decisively place the most trust in professional food writers

D) readers have increasingly come to trust professional food writers

Results of a 2018 Poll (Scientific) of New York Residents

Most Frequently Visited Information Source

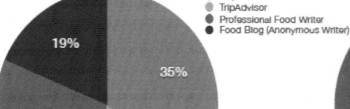

- Yelp
- TripAdvisor
- Professional Food Writer
- Food Blog (Anonymous Writer)

19%
35%
28%
19%

Most Trusted Information Source

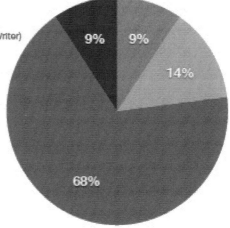

9% 9%
14%
68%

CONTINUE

Professional food journalists are seasoned writers who contribute to publications, newsletters, or blogs. Journalists of this sort often **14** has knowledge of a wide range of cuisines, modes of food preparation, and ingredients used in dishes. A given writer may write a review article that rates the quality of a meal, or might bring forth information about specific restaurants or foods. Some food writers specialize in articles about types of cuisine that may include ethnic meals, desserts, spirits, **15** foods, for specialized diets, and comfort food.

Restaurants frequently hire executive chefs who curate the menu, source ingredients, and oversee the daily operations of a kitchen. Writers like to include information about chefs, their career backgrounds, and the restaurants where these chefs have worked; thus, readers can know what to expect from the cuisine. An efficient and effective food writer will **16** undertake or perform a considerable amount of research before writing an article.

14
A) NO CHANGE
B) have knowledge
C) had knowledge
D) were having knowledge

15
A) NO CHANGE
B) foods for specialized, diets, and comfort food.
C) foods for specialized diets, and comfort food.
D) foods; for specialized diets and comfort food.

16
A) NO CHANGE
B) perform a considerable amount of research
C) perform a considerable, large quantity of research
D) undertake it

Test 2

Like fashion and music, food is subject to ever-changing trends. Whether the coverage [17] concerns craft burgers, plant-based diets, gluten free choices, organic foods, or all-natural sweeteners, there is always something inventive happening on the food scene. A food writer must stay [18] abreast to new developments to write authoritatively and to keep his or her readers informed.

[19] Creativity and spontaneity are essential to being a successful food writer. Writers are frequently in contact with public relations firms that represent restaurants. These firms issue press releases that provide up-to-date information about restaurant openings, staff changes, menu updates, and special events. Public relations firms communicate with food writers so that the restaurants that they are working for will be written about.

17

A) NO CHANGE
B) instigates
C) gets to
D) calls upon

18

A) NO CHANGE
B) abreast on
C) abreast of
D) abreast with

19

The writer is considering deleting the underlined sentence. Should the underlined content be kept or deleted?

A) Kept, because justifies the earlier argument that food writers should reach out to specific readers.

B) Kept, because it introduces skills that are explained in different forms in the paragraph.

C) Deleted, because the writer never argues that creativity is the most important ability for food writers.

D) Deleted, because the paragraph addresses a set of activities that are not reflected in the sentence.

CONTINUE →

Journalists often write in depth about the region where a restaurant is located because factors such as geography [20] effect the quality of food that is served. For example, the farm-to-table movement can guide the menu at a restaurant that sources fruits, vegetables, meats, fish, and cheeses locally. Restaurants that use such local sourcing change their menus frequently. The movement [21] support small farmers and community businesses while ensuring that guests get the freshest foods possible.

Though built on enjoyment, the restaurant industry is competitive and consumers have many choices when they dine out. [22] In order to navigate such a large array of options, restaurant-goers rely on dependable food journalists to convey accurate information that facilitates rewarding meal experiences.

20

A) NO CHANGE
B) affect
C) effects
D) affects

21

A) NO CHANGE
B) supports
C) supported
D) had supported

22

Which choice provides information that best reflects the writer's ideas?

A) NO CHANGE
B) To help the most popular restaurants to continue to thrive,
C) Even while working as food journalists themselves,
D) Faced with such confusing and unpleasant prospects,

CONTINUE

Questions 23-33 are based on the following passage.

The Orangutan: An Animal with "Culture"

From culture to culture, small points of etiquette can differ considerably. This idea holds true not only for the various human cultures that interest anthropologists, [23] or also for the identifiable "cultures" that arise among advanced primate species. Consider the orangutan, a species that ranges over the island nations of southeast Asia. These large, tree-based apes are known for their problem-solving capacities, including their ability to use tools.

However, did you also know that some tool usages differ [24] considerably: from one orangutan grouping to the next. According to the conservation agency Orangutan Foundation International, orangutans use leaves as a mealtime implement: while some orangutan cultures [25] have adopted practical uses for leaves, others primarily use leaves to carry and handle prickly, edible vegetables.

23

A) NO CHANGE

B) but also

C) and also

D) DELETE the underlined portion.

24

A) NO CHANGE

B) considerably, from one orangutan grouping to the next.

C) considerably: from one orangutan grouping to the next?

D) considerably from one orangutan grouping to the next?

25

Which choice adds the most logical and effective supporting detail to the writer's discussion?

A) NO CHANGE

B) designate leaves for use as napkins,

C) employ leaves for various "cleaning" tasks,

D) are averse to practical uses for leaves,

CONTINUE

Specialists in animal behavior are still examining the full array of ways in which orangutan culture expresses [26] itself, a task where it can be complicated because orangutans, rather than forming large social units, are solitary animals. Yet in the past few years, biologists and fieldworkers [27] have diligently gathered data that serve, altogether, as a multi-faceted validation of orangutan culture.

26

A) NO CHANGE

B) itself, a task in which it

C) itself, a task which

D) itself a task that

27

A) NO CHANGE

B) would have diligently gathered

C) will diligently gather

D) diligently gather

CONTINUE

Test 2

[1] One of the most important studies of orangutan customs emerged from Duke University in 2003. [2] The researchers **28** <u>enmeshed therein</u> reported that, in addition to adopting practical "customs" that differed from region to region, orangutans engaged in non-practical behaviors that differentiated one orangutan culture from another. [3] For example, some orangutan groups engaged in a rudimentary sport called "snag riding." [4] In this recreation, orangutans will grasp onto dying, destabilized trunks and ride the falling trees down to the forest floor. [5] **29** <u>Each stick</u> out their lips and emit distinctive "raspberry" blowing sounds, to borrow the human expression. **30**

28

A) NO CHANGE

B) behind this endeavor

C) there to keep the work happening

D) making this all go smoothly

29

A) NO CHANGE

B) A group stick

C) Another orangutan sticks

D) Other orangutans stick

30

The writer wishes to add the following sentence to this paragraph.

> Some displays of orangutan culture, however, do not entail such dramatic activities.

To make the order of ideas most logical, the best placement for this content would be after

A) sentence 2.

B) sentence 3.

C) sentence 4.

D) sentence 5.

CONTINUE

After establishing the reality of orangutan culture, researchers then began to investigate the mechanisms by which such culture could be generated and transmitted. Logging over 100,000 hours of data from over 150 orangutans, a 2011 University of Zurich study **[31]** prophesied that orangutans would adapt their customs as their surroundings changed. Co-author Carel van Schaik, **[32]** who was also involved, in the 2003 study, attributed such a breakthrough in understanding to "the unprecedented size of our dataset." Such a dataset also provided firm reinforcement for the intuitive parallels between orangutans and humans. **[33]** Exactly as humans might develop a specific style of either heat-retaining or self-ventilating architecture depending on climate, orangutans might adapt their customs to the foliage or food supplies of an area. Yet the exact interplay of genetic influences and environmental influences that determines orangutan customs has yet to be determined. For scientists, the appreciation of orangutan culture has only begun.

31
A) NO CHANGE
B) started saying that
C) concluded that
D) finished that

32
A) NO CHANGE
B) who was, also involved, in the 2003 study attributed
C) who was also involved in the 2003 study, attributed
D) who was also involved in the 2003 study attributed

33
A) NO CHANGE
B) Although
C) More than
D) Much as

CONTINUE

Test 2

Questions 34-44 are based on the following passage.

A Guided Tour of New York Film History

On Location Tours is a bus tour company that has been operating for over 18 years in the New York metropolitan area; by design, this company presents opportunities for people to experience New York City from a wholly different perspective. Even native New Yorkers will learn a great deal about [34] their city: when they take an On Location themed tour through the Big Apple. [35]

34

A) NO CHANGE

B) their city; when

C) their city when

D) their city. When

35

At this point, the writer is considering inserting the following sentence.

> Moreover, because the typical tour is easy to book and is quite affordable, On Location Tours has natural advantages over its competitors.

Should the writer make this insertion here?

A) Yes, because it addresses and refutes a criticism of On Location Tours.

B) Yes, because it gives greater clarity to the writer's main argument.

C) No, because it focuses on a topic that is not pursued elsewhere in the passage.

D) No, because it detracts from the writer's positive stance regarding On Location Tours.

CONTINUE

[1] One such offering is the Classic Film Tour, which occurs every Saturday morning and introduces all who have joined to New York sites where great works of cinema were shot on-location. [2] A three- to four-hour excursion on a comfortable coach bus originates in the vibrant Times Square area. [3] **36** An individual with assigned duties, such as a guide, mentions locations of interest while guests observe film clips on monitors that **37** point at iconic buildings and sites. [4] Over 30 individual places—including museums, hotels, and performing arts centers—are presented along with **38** its relationship to specific classic movies. [5] The tour bus also courses through Manhattan neighborhoods that include the Upper West Side, the Upper East Side, and Midtown, so that the tour extends well beyond consideration of major landmarks. [6] There are even opportunities to disembark from this vehicle to capture photographs. **39**

36

Which choice provides a precise description that helps to support the writer's tone regarding the Classic Film Tour?

A) NO CHANGE

B) A guide who possesses obscure film knowledge

C) A guide who may or may not be a film expert

D) A well-informed and personable guide

37

A) NO CHANGE

B) embrace

C) highlight

D) unearth

38

A) NO CHANGE

B) one's relationship

C) our relationship

D) their relationship

39

To make this paragraph most logical, sentence 5 should be placed

A) where it is now.

B) after sentence 1.

C) after sentence 3.

D) after sentence 6.

CONTINUE

This tour is sponsored by Turner Classic Movies (TCM), a company that—despite the "classic" label—actually preserves and promotes a variety of popular cinematic works. Classic movies are not necessarily old films: they are, instead, distinctive films [40] that, whether long-lived or not, have gained substantial followings.

[41] On a TCM Classic Film Tour, even familiar landmarks in New York City assume a new significance. While the Plaza Hotel is the most commonly filmed building in the city, Central Park, another tour site, has been in more [42] movies' than any other place in the world. The Queensboro Bridge, also known as the 59th Street Bridge, was constructed in 1901. Because of its long history, it was seen in both the 1936 film *My Man Godfrey* and 43 years later in a more recent production, Woody Allen's 1979 movie *Manhattan*.

40

A) NO CHANGE

B) that earn the "classic" label by having gained large followings.

C) that are followed by large, substantial numbers of viewers.

D) that have gained substantial followings.

41

Which choice best sets up the information provided in the paragraph that follows?

A) NO CHANGE

B) Two TCM Classic Film Tours that take place on the same day may travel to different locations.

C) In general, a TCM Classic Film Tour will avoid obvious landmarks for more subtle sites of interest.

D) The typical TCM Classic Film Tour assumes some knowledge of cinema on the part of its participants.

42

A) NO CHANGE

B) movies than any other place

C) movies' than any place

D) movies than any place

CONTINUE

Another site, Tiffany's, is a renowned jewelry store on the corner of 5th Avenue and 57th Street. The 1961 melodrama *Breakfast at Tiffany's* starred Audrey Hepburn in the role of Holly Golightly, who was depicted standing outside the upscale shop. A more interesting element of the tour showcases a site many blocks away on East 71st Street, **43** for whom a series of outdoor shots were filmed to indicate that Golightly "lived" in one of the street's brownstones.

Ordinarily, city tours are designed for tourists who are just **44** passing through, however, the TCM Classic Movie Film Tour is designed to cater to native New Yorkers who may not know of the wealth of film history hiding in plain sight.

43
A) NO CHANGE
B) which
C) where
D) when

44
A) NO CHANGE
B) passing through. However, the TCM
C) passing through, however the TCM
D) passing. Through, however, the TCM

STOP

If you finish before time is called, you may check your work on this section only.
Do not turn to any other section.

Answer Key: Test 2

Passage 1		Passage 2		Passage 3		Passage 4	
1.	A	12.	C	23.	B	34.	C
2.	B	13.	C	24.	D	35.	C
3.	B	14.	B	25.	B	36.	D
4.	C	15.	C	26.	C	37.	C
5.	D	16.	B	27.	A	38.	D
6.	B	17.	A	28.	B	39.	A
7.	D	18.	C	29.	D	40.	D
8.	B	19.	D	30.	C	41.	A
9.	C	20.	B	31.	C	42.	B
10.	B	21.	B	32.	C	43.	C
11.	D	22.	A	33.	D	44.	B

Topic Areas by Question

Expression of Ideas

Passage 1: Questions 1-3, 6, 9, 11

Passage 2: Questions 12-13, 16-17, 19, 22

Passage 3, Questions 24-25, 28, 30-31, 33

Passage 4, Questions 35-37, 39-41

Standard English Conventions

Passage 1: Questions 4-5, 7-8, 10

Passage 2: Questions 14-15, 18, 20-21

Passage 3, Questions 23, 26-27, 29, 32

Passage 4, Questions 34, 38, 42-44

Answer Explanations
Test 2, Pages 28-43

Passage 1, Pages 28-31

1. <u>A</u> is the correct answer.

The goal in this question is to set up the rest of the passage, which is about birdwatching and the National Audubon Society. The first sentence gives a simplistic view of birdwatching, and so the sentence at hand needs to imply more complexity. Thus, A is right. B is unsupported, while C and D are too informal and are excessively negative in tone.

2. <u>B</u> is the correct answer.

Officials are in charge of chapter administration, so they SUPERVISE chapters. Thus, B is right. "Accumulate" means to gather, "pursue" means to chase, and "scan" means to look at briefly; none of those options make sense here.

3. <u>B</u> is the correct answer.

Citizen scientists must be performing scientific functions. Thus, gathering data (choice B) is correct. A is irrelevant, while C and D are vague and would better refer to broad moral or ethical issues as well.

4. <u>C</u> is the correct answer.

The choices for this question differ only in their punctuation, so this is a punctuation question. This is a list, and so the items should be separated by commas with the word "and" preceding the last item in the list. Thus, C is right. A and B have extra words, while D omits the "and."

5. <u>D</u> is the correct answer.

D is right because no punctuation is needed. Colons do not interrupt phrases, so eliminate B and C. A is wrong because "studying the ongoing status and ranges of bird populations across the Americas" is a modifier of "researchers," and so it should not be separated from "researchers" by a colon.

6. <u>B</u> is the correct answer.

The title of the graph shows that the graph is about the number of birdwatchers in the U.S., so B is right. A is about the number of birdwatching excursions, which isn't recorded in the graph. C is wrong because birdwatching away from home exceeded birdwatching near home in every year shown, so it doesn't make sense to say that birdwatching away from home is becoming as popular as birdwatching near home. D is wrong because it concerns the future, which isn't depicted in the graph.

7. <u>D</u> is the correct answer.

The antecedent (noun) for the pronoun is "people." That antecedent is plural, so D (they) is right. The words provided in A, B, and C are singular, so that these choices are automatically wrong.

8. <u>B</u> is the correct answer.

The correct phrasing is "contributes . . . to," so B is right. A, C, and D each use the wrong preposition, and thus break an idiomatic phrase that can only take the preposition "to" in standard English.

9. <u>C</u> is the correct answer.

The goal here is to transition to the notion that the "Rio Grand Valley features scenic tourist destinations." Thus, it is necessary to mention the scenic nature of the Rio Grand Valley. C is the only choice ("alluring natural landscape") that does. A (finances), B (revitalization), and D (finances) all place emphasis on features other than the attractive tourism-oriented aspects of the area itself.

10. <u>B</u> is the correct answer.

Because there is a comma before the underlined text, we cannot create two sentences. B is right because it doesn't create two sentences and is consistently plural. D is wrong because "each" is singular while "spots" is plural. A and C are comma splices (two independent clauses joined by a comma).

11. <u>D</u> is the correct answer.

The three activities listed are all "intriguing ways to participate in modern birdwatching." Thus, D is right because it indicates that any one of the three activities is an intriguing way to participate in modern birdwatching." The other three choices indicate contrast, i.e. that the three activities listed are NOT intriguing ways to participate in modern birdwatching.

Passage 2, Pages 32-35

12. C is the correct answer.

That "these reviews can vary widely depending on individual experiences" agrees with "are often very subjective." Thus, C (and) is right. B (but) indicates contrast, while A and D are illogical and create awkward constructions that appear to refer back to "experience," not to "reviews."

13. C is the correct answer.

All of the answer choices are about trust, so the "most trusted information source" pie chart is the relevant chart for this question. The sector for professional food writers is much larger than the other sectors, and so C is right. A, B, and D are outside the scope of what is shown in the chart. Don't be fooled by A; the percentages in the chart are the percentages of respondents who listed that option as their most trusted, NOT the percentages of people in that source that are trusted.

14. B is the correct answer.

The words "journalists are" in the prior sentence show that the present tense is appropriate. Moreover, "journalists" is a plural word. B is right because "have" is the plural present tense of the verb "to have." A is singular, while C and D are past tense.

15. C is the correct answer.

The choices for this question differ only in their punctuation, so this is a punctuation question. This is a list, and so the items should be separated by commas with the word "and" preceding the last item in the list. Thus, C is right. A, B, and D all have extra punctuation marks.

16. B is the correct answer.

B is right because it provides the needed information without being redundant. A and C are redundant, adding un-needed synonyms for "perform" and "considerable," while D doesn't specify what "it" is.

17. A is the correct answer.

This is a word choice question, so it is helpful to come up with your own word to substitute for the underlined word. Coverage IS ABOUT a topic, so the question requires an answer that means "is about." A is the only match, while B, C, and D break this standard English idiom.

18. <u>C</u> is the correct answer.

The correct phrasing is "stay abreast of" (meaning "stay aware of") and so C is right. The other three choices use the wrong preposition, and for this reason should be eliminated as departing from standard English usage.

19. <u>D</u> is the correct answer.

The paragraph as a whole features a discussion of how writers connect with or network with public relations firms; a discussion of "creativity and spontaneity" as more general qualities is not directly or effectively related to this topic. Choose D and eliminate A (since the sentence does not clearly mention readers) and B (since the sentence is off-topic in relation to the paragraph. C presents a reason for deletion (what the writer thinks of creativity) that is irrelevant, since creativity is not the paragraph's focus in any case.

20. <u>B</u> is the correct answer.

"Affect" is a verb in this sentence, so "affect" (not "effect," which is a noun) is the correct spelling. The subject (factors) is plural so we need to use the plural form of the verb, which is "affect" rather than "affects." Thus, B is right.

21. <u>B</u> is the correct answer.

The verbs in the prior sentence show that the present tense is needed for agreement. Moreover, "the movement" is a singular subject. B is right because "supports" is the singular present tense of the verb "to support" A is plural, while C and D are past tense.

22. <u>A</u> is the correct answer.

The goal is to support the positive idea that "consumers have many choices when they dine out." Thus, A is right. B (popularity) and C (people working) are off-topic, while D is negative.

Passage 3, Pages 36-39

23. <u>B</u> is the correct answer.

Just as "neither" and "nor" constitute a word pair, "not only" and "but also" form a pair. Thus, B is correct. A and C have the wrong first word, while D omits the second part of the pair altogether.

24. <u>D</u> is the correct answer.

This sentence is a question, so eliminate A and B and consider C and D. D is correct because "differ . . . from" is a paired phrase and thus should not be interrupted by punctuation (which is also why C is wrong).

25. <u>B</u> is the correct answer.

The goal here is to support the idea of using leaves as mealtime implements. Thus, the answer should describe a mealtime use for leaves, and so B is correct. The other choices don't describe a mealtime use for leaves, even though they do appear to reference the practical uses that leaves are put to in OTHER contexts.

26. <u>C</u> is the correct answer.

C is the correct choice because it uses a comma to separate an independent clause from a dependent one and does not introduce unnecessary words. The word "itself" ends a clause, so there needs to be a comma after that word (eliminate D). The words "where" and "in which" are for locations, which are not referenced here, so eliminate A and B.

27. <u>A</u> is the correct answer.

This is a verb question. The sentence is about what biologists and field workers have been doing in "the past few years," so the verb should be in the past perfect tense (i.e. past tense of the main verb preceded by "have"). Thus, A is correct. B, C, and D are the wrong tenses (subjunctive, future, and present, respectively).

28. <u>B</u> is the correct answer.

The researchers are responsible for conducting the studies. Thus, B is the best wording. C and D are too informal, while choice A (indicating that the researchers are trapped) does not make sense.

29. <u>D</u> is the correct answer.

This paragraph discusses groups of orangutans. Thus, the subject is plural. Choice D is correct, while the other three choices use singular subjects. Do not be fooled by choice B: "a group" is grammatically singular.

30. <u>C</u> is the correct answer.

Sentences 3 and 4 describe "snag riding," while sentence 5 describes sounds that the orangutans make. Thus, the proposed sentence should go between sentences 4 and 5 to transition between the raucous, or "dramatic," activity of snag riding and the stationary activity of making blowing sounds.

31. <u>C</u> is the correct answer.

The study reached a conclusion after the scientists analyzed data, and the underlined portion should reflect this context of analysis and findings. Thus, C is correct. A is possibly too formal and in any case relates to predictions, while B (related to speech) and D (ending or disregarding a process) have the wrong meaning.

32. <u>C</u> is the correct answer.

The phrase "who was also involved in the 2003 study" is a side-comment (which can be deleted and still yield a fully functional sentence), so it should be set off with two commas. Thus, C is correct. A and B cut that phrase with a comma, while D is missing a comma.

33. <u>D</u> is the correct answer.

This sentence describes an analogy between human and orangutan adaptations to their environments. Thus, D is correct because it indicates similarity though not (on account of the different species) complete interchangeability. B and C indicate difference, while A states that human and orangutan behaviors are identical, which isn't what the writer is saying.

Passage 4, Pages 40-43

34. <u>C</u> is the correct answer.

There is no pause or separation of ideas between the text before "when" and the text after it. Thus, no punctuation is needed and so C is correct. "When they take an On Location themed tour through the Big Apple" is not a sentence. Thus, eliminate B and D. Choice A incorrectly uses a colon.

35. <u>C</u> is the correct answer.

The indented sentence is about On Location's advantages over its competitors. That is not relevant to the paragraph, so the sentence shouldn't be added. Eliminate A and B and choose C. D is wrong because the sentence isn't negative, so it does not detract from the writer's positive stance.

36. <u>D</u> is the correct answer.

The goal is this question is to support he writer's tone, which is positive, with precise information. D is right because it is positive and descriptive. A (neutral), B (possibly negative), and C (possibly negative) are not clearly positive in the same manner.

37. <u>C</u> is the correct answer.

This is a word choice question, so it is helpful to come up with your own word to substitute for the underlined word. The tour's film clips DRAW ATTENTION TO the iconic sights of the city. Thus, we need a word that means "to draw attention to." C is the only choice that fits, while the other choices are best suited to describing physical actions performed by people.

38. D is the correct answer.

The phrase between the dashes can be deleted, so read the sentence without it to find the subject. The subject is "places," which is third-person plural. Thus, we need a plural pronoun, so D is the only acceptable answer.

39. A is the correct answer.

The earlier part of the paragraph describes the landmarks on the tour, while sentence 5 states that the tour "also courses through" other areas, so that the tour extends "beyond . . . landmarks." Thus, sentence 5 should go after all of the sentences that are about landmarks, which means that it must go after sentence 4. Thus, A is right and B and C are wrong. D is wrong because sentence 6 switches to a new topic (places to disembark from the bus), and so sentence 5 must go before it.

40. D is the correct answer.

D is right because it is the only answer that isn't redundant. The first part of A is redundant with "not necessarily old films." The first part of B is redundant with "Classic movies." "Large" and "substantial" in C are redundant.

41. A is the correct answer.

The rest of the paragraph explains the significance of New York landmarks as they relate to a TCM tour. Thus, A is the best introduction to that content. B and D don't mention landmarks, while C isn't true because the paragraph makes reference to "obvious" or popular locations as elements of the tour.

42. B is the correct answer.

The word "movies" is a noun in this sentence, so the correct form is "movies" rather than "movies' ". Central Park has been in more movies than OTHER places have. Thus, B is right. A and C use the possessive form (movies'), while D is an incorrect comparison (since Central Park was not in more movies than itself, only in more movies than OTHER places were).

43. C is the correct answer.

The underlined portion should designate a place of filming for the "outdoor shots." Choose C, because "where," is the proper pronoun to indicate a place. A (whom) involves an object pronoun that can only indicate a person, B (which) normally indicates a thing, and D (when) normally indicates time.

44. B is the correct answer.

This is a punctuation question, so check to see if there are really two sentences here. There are, and the end of the first one is "through," so that B is right. D puts the period in the wrong place and cuts the phrase "passing through" with a period. A and C are run-on sentences.

Test 3

Writing and Language

2018 SAT Practice

Test 3

Writing and Language Test

35 MINUTES, 44 QUESTIONS

Turn to Section 2 of your answer sheet to answer the questions in this section.

Questions 1-11 are based on the following passage.

Gregor Mendel: The Father of Modern Genetics

Gregor Johann Mendel (1822-1884) was a friar in a region of the Austrian Empire that is now known as the Czech Republic. By performing painstaking experiments for eight years in his monastery's garden, **1** his discovery was the basis of genetic inheritance. He accomplished this feat by studying *Pisum sativum*,

1

A) NO CHANGE

B) he discovered the basis of genetic inheritance.

C) the basis of genetic inheritance was his discovery.

D) genetic inheritance was discovered in its basis by him.

the common pea plant. Sadly, the significance of his work went largely unnoticed during [2] his lifetime, although his documents were rediscovered decades later by other scientists and eventually became the basis of modern genetics.

Mendel studied seven binary traits (i.e. traits having exactly two versions): pod shape, pod color, seed shape, seed color, plant height, flower position, and flower color. [3] Ironically, the two versions of pea color are green and yellow, without any gradations or "halfway" options. Similarly, humans either have the Rh factor in their blood (they are Rh+) or they don't (they are Rh-); [4] Mendel did not consider any other possibilities.

2

A) NO CHANGE
B) his lifetime although, his documents
C) his lifetime; although his documents
D) his lifetime, although; his documents

3

A) NO CHANGE
B) Conversely,
C) In retrospect,
D) For example,

4

Which choice best supports the writer's characterization of binary traits?

A) NO CHANGE
B) other elements of human genetics are more difficult to analyze.
C) there is no intermediate option.
D) this is the current consensus.

CONTINUE

Test 3

The predominant theory of Mendel's time was that of Blending Inheritance, which posited that the traits of offspring were intermediate versions of their parents' traits. If the Blending Inheritance theory [5] was correct, crossing green and yellow peas with each other would result in greenish-yellow peas. However, when Mendel [6] has performed that cross, all of the resulting offspring were yellow. Because all of the offspring must have inherited one yellow allele (version of a gene) from their yellow parent and one green allele from their green parent, Mendel reasoned that the yellow allele (Y) must mask the effects of the green allele (y). [7] Mendel named this phenomenon "dominance." The allele that gets masked is called the recessive allele and the allele that masks it is called the dominant allele.

5

A) NO CHANGE
B) is correct
C) are correct
D) were correct

6

A) NO CHANGE
B) performs
C) performed
D) performing

7

The writer is considering deleting the underlined sentence. Should this content be kept or deleted?

A) Kept, because the term "dominance" appears prominently in later paragraphs.
B) Kept, because the idea of "dominance" is central to Mendel's logic.
C) Deleted, because it places emphasis on an idea that the passage later dismisses.
D) Deleted, because it interrupts the explanation of Mendel's experimental process.

CONTINUE

After observing that all of the offspring from his cross were yellow, Mendel crossed two of those offspring with each other. When Mendel tallied the results of the second cross, he found that [8] the resulting generation of either green or yellow specimens consisted of approximately 75% yellow plants and 25% green plants. These percentages confirmed Mendel's theory that the yellow allele masks the green allele. The YY (25%) and Yy (50%) peas were yellow. Only the yy peas (25%) [9] were green. These peas had no Y allele to mask their recessive y alleles.

The gene inheritance patterns of many humans are more complex [10] than the pea plants that Mendel studied. [11] Mendel is perhaps the most famous scientist who also pursued a religious vocation, and so Mendel's work has been immensely influential in the understanding of how humans inherit traits from their parents. From that understanding have come many medical breakthroughs that have improved the lives of countless people.

8

A) NO CHANGE
B) those plants which were part of its outcome
C) the resulting generation
D) those of them

9

Which choice best combines the sentences at the underlined portion, and best reflects Mendel's ideas about the pea plants?

A) were green, because they
B) were green, although they
C) were green; as a result, they
D) were green; later on, they

10

A) NO CHANGE
B) than each of the pea plants
C) than those of the pea plants
D) than the complexity of the pea plants

11

Which choice provides the most logical explanation for the information presented in the later portion of the sentence?

A) NO CHANGE
B) The implications of Mendel's work were not foreseen by Mendel himself,
C) All inheritance patters have the same underpinnings,
D) Scientists today continue to delve into Mendel's writings,

CONTINUE

Test 3

Questions 12-22 are based on the following passage and supplementary material.

Shining a New Light on Historic Lighthouses

Before there were any electronic devices, lighthouses were one of the essential navigation tools used by boats and ships. Lighthouses help vessels maintain to safe travel when these vessels are near land formations. They also help ship navigators to precisely determine their positions. **12** A lighthouse can be a stone residence, a tower, or another type of building that houses a high-intensity lamp designed to cast a bright light. Lighthouses have long functioned much like traffic **13** signals, as they operate instead on waterways. Even though there has been **14** a fearsome swelter of technological development in the past several decades, the United States Coast Guard recognizes that old-fashioned lighthouses assist navigation.

12

At this point, the writer is considering adding the following sentence to the passage.

Indeed, sailors and mariners would often find reassurance in the appearance of a lighthouse after a long voyage.

Should the writer insert this content?

A) Yes, because it helps to explain why lighthouses were considered useful.

B) Yes, because it provides a reason for the construction of lighthouses.

C) No, because it raises a topic that is loosely related to the practical functioning of lighthouses.

D) No, because its needlessly elevated style distracts from the writer's analysis.

13

A) NO CHANGE

B) indicators, or signals, on waterways.

C) signals on waterways over time.

D) signals on waterways.

14

A) NO CHANGE

B) an amazing back-and-forth

C) an impressive pace

D) a hugeness

CONTINUE

The first lighthouse in America was built in 1716 on Little Brewster Island in Boston, Massachusetts. However, the oldest existing lighthouse in the United States, which never had to be rebuilt, is situated in Sandy Hook, New Jersey. Originally constructed 1764, the Sandy Hook Lighthouse is still operational. Over 1,500 lighthouses were constructed in the U.S., **15** but there were no more than 450 working at any one time. While many think that lighthouses would be confined to coastal states, 267 were constructed on the shores of the Great Lakes. **16** At one time, Michigan had the most lighthouses with a total of 140; Maine was also the site of many lighthouses, with approximately 80 structures in 1994.

Total Number of Lighthouses in the United States

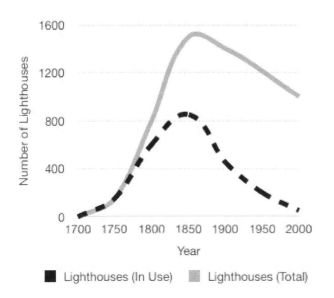

15

Which choice best reflects the data in the graph?

A) NO CHANGE

B) but there were no more than 850 working at any one time.

C) and a majority of them were working at any one time.

D) and at least 200 of them were working at any one time.

16

The writer would like to include a statement that accurately reflects the information in the following tables, as well as the data in the graph.

States with the Most Lighthouses (1974)

State	Ranking	Lighthouses
Michigan	1	140
Maine	2	85
Massachusetts	3	63

States with the Most Lighthouses (1994)

State	Ranking	Lighthouses
Maine	1	82
Michigan	2	78
Massachusetts	3	57

Which choice accomplishes this goal?

A) Over a twenty-year period, Michigan had more lighthouses than did all other states combined

B) At one time, Michigan had more lighthouses than did all other states combined

C) Over a twenty-year period, Michigan had the most lighthouses of any state

D) At one time, Michigan had the most lighthouses of any state

Test 3

Lighthouses are [17] builtly typical of strong materials that include wood, granite, brick, sandstone, steel, cast iron, and reinforced concrete. However, because these structures are located along shorelines, harsh weather conditions can erode even the most durable building materials. For this reason, many lighthouses have had to be refurbished, while some have been completely rebuilt.

[18] Because lighthouses were seldom constructed to endure, many lighthouses have fallen to disuse and some have even faced demolition. The United States has instituted the National Historic Lighthouse Preservation Act of 2000. It allows for lighthouse structures to be made available to local governments [19] and of private non-profit organizations. There are also associations with dedicated members that have been formed to restore and save lighthouses; [20] one of these groups is the United States Lighthouse Society.

CONTINUE

17

A) NO CHANGE
B) built, and typical
C) builtly and typically
D) typically built

18

Which choice provides the most logical introduction to the writer's explanation in this sentence?

A) NO CHANGE
B) Though mostly owned by state governments,
C) Perhaps best known today as tourist attractions,
D) As navigation systems have been modernized,

19

A) NO CHANGE
B) and to private non-profit organizations.
C) and for private non-profit organizations.
D) and there are private non-profit organizations.

20

A) NO CHANGE
B) one of these groups are
C) one of these groups being
D) one of these being

Lighthouses are considered [21] unique elements in the national history of the United States and have become popular tourist attractions. Our National Park system features ones that include The Bass Harbor Headlight at Acadia National Park in Maine, Alcatraz Island Light on Alcatraz Island in the San Francisco Bay of California, and the Boca Chita Lighthouse at Biscayne National Park in Florida. Visitors to these and other sites have the chance to learn about the buildings' [22] backgrounds, and they enter the lighthouses, and climb the towers to see sweeping views of the local landscapes.

21

A) NO CHANGE

B) unique elements in the history of the United States

C) unique elements as aspects of the history of the United States

D) unique aspects in the history, as happening over time, of the United States

22

A) NO CHANGE

B) backgrounds and enter the lighthouses, and they climb the towers

C) backgrounds, enter the lighthouses, and climb the towers

D) backgrounds, the lighthouses, and climb the towers

CONTINUE

Test 3

Questions 23-33 are based on the following passage.

The Lyrical Prose of Yasunari Kawabata

In 1968, Yasunari Kawabata became the first author of Japanese descent to be granted the world-renowned Nobel Prize in Literature. [23] The Nobel Foundation, in its announcement of the award commended Kawabata in particular for his "narrative mastery, which with great sensibility expresses the essence of the Japanese mind." His best works succeed in transporting their readers to a Japanese landscape rich with the beauties of nature and the glories of Japanese culture, [24] or do so in a manner that—at least at first—can be rather disorienting.

23

A) NO CHANGE
B) The Nobel Foundation in its announcement of the award,
C) The Nobel Foundation in its announcement, of the award
D) The Nobel Foundation, in its announcement of the award,

24

A) NO CHANGE
B) to
C) yet
D) and

CONTINUE

[1] A newcomer to Kawabata may, in fact, be left with the impression that [25] they have just read through random snippets of experience tied together with thrilling observations of setting and emotion.

[2] In Kawabata's *Snow Country* (1937), a man named Shimamura [26] frequents a scenic resort town in the chilly region of Japan that gives the novel its title; here, he tries and for the most part fails to form meaningful human connections during his excursions. [3] The novel concludes, abruptly, with Shimamura's observations both of a building that has caught on fire in the night and of the mystical Milky Way above. [4] Another Kawabata novel, *The Sound of the Mountain* (1949), follows a similarly puzzling template. [5] In this work, an aging man named Shingo reflects on his disappointing family life and occasionally finds solace in observations of natural life, such as the [27] jaw-dropping sunflowers that grow in his neighborhood. [6] He does not, however, bring his disappointments to a point of crisis or change that a reader waiting for a standard climax might expect. [7] The typical Kawabata novel may not seem like a fully-developed narrative on an initial read-through. [28]

25

A) NO CHANGE
B) we have
C) it has
D) he or she has

26

A) NO CHANGE
B) situates
C) accommodates
D) has effective going with

27

Which choice best maintains the style and tone of the passage?

A) NO CHANGE
B) flagrantly cogent
C) majestic
D) insane

28

To make the order of ideas in the paragraph most logical, sentence 7 should be placed

A) where it is now.
B) before sentence 1.
C) after sentence 3.
D) after sentence 4.

CONTINUE

To see the seemingly haphazard nature of a Kawabata narrative as an artistic flaw is [29] missing the point of Kawabata's approach to the novel. What Kawabata aspires to capture is exactly the randomness and unpredictability of human experience; in his novels as in life, [30] there is no grand "plots" but a chain of occurrences that urge us to contemplation. In terms of Shingo, for instance, the real question is not "What will happen to this man?" but "Why has this man accepted a life of unhappiness?" The second question cuts deeper into how Shingo [31] thinks.

29

A) NO CHANGE
B) to miss the point
C) what misses the point
D) that which misses the point

30

A) NO CHANGE
B) there are
C) there was
D) there being

31

The writer wishes to revise the underlined portion so that this sentence reflects the passage's ideas about Shingo as a character. Which choice best accomplishes this goal?

A) thinks, and prompts further consideration of the possible emotion-laden parallels between Shingo and Kawabata himself.

B) thinks, and perhaps inspires readers to approach the text with questions of their own

C) thinks, and urges readers to consider why Shingo cannot look beyond his family to counter-act his life of melancholy.

D) thinks, and reinforces the sense that Kawabata's narratives require re-reading to become fully understandable.

CONTINUE

It is no surprise that, with his fragmentary style and powers of observation, Kawabata crafted uniquely-formatted short [32] narratives. The "palm-of-the-hand" stories, intriguing texts that are only two or three pages long. [33] Even though Kawabata's novels may be destined to be forgotten, his poignant shorter works have ensured him a prominent place in literary history.

32

A) NO CHANGE
B) narratives the
C) narratives; the
D) narratives: the

33

Which of the following, as a concluding sentence for the passage, best reflects the writer's characterization of Kawabata?

A) NO CHANGE

B) Often, these accounts focus on exciting childhood memories, demonstrating that Kawabata himself did not succumb to Shingo's and Shimamura's pessimism.

C) Acclaimed for such fiction today, Kawabata continues to inspire innovative novelists worldwide.

D) As an efficient yet powerful observer of human nature, Kawabata captured the "Japanese mind" while urging all readers to think deeply.

CONTINUE

Test 3

When the Workforce Grows Old

[34] With the American workforce employing historically large numbers of older (60 years and over) employees, young workers find themselves facing a series of difficult alternatives. As they would in any era, retiring older workers will be faced with the challenge of staying healthy and sociable as they leave workplaces that sometimes function as small communities. Maintaining a fulfilling and active lifestyle in [35] retirement; however, may be uniquely difficult in the early 21st century. Recent statistics have revealed that 36% of workers over the age of 55 have saved less than $10,000. A small fraction of the roughly $60,000 that the average United States household earns every year, this amount saved is surely inadequate to offer [36] financial security to a retiree who is no longer employed.

34

Which sentence provides the most effective introduction to the writer's discussion in this paragraph?

A) NO CHANGE

B) A variety of demographic and economic trends related to the aging of the American workforce will make the decades ahead difficult for even the most experienced employees.

C) In the face of increased economic instability, America's "aging" workforce has become the subject of one of the most contentious sociological debates of modern times.

D) Though regarded by many as elements of an unforeseen crisis, the converging difficulties that face the oldest workers (60 years and over) in the United States are the end results of well-documented historical trends.

35

A) NO CHANGE

B) retirement, however; may be

C) retirement, however, may be

D) retirement, however may be

36

A) NO CHANGE

B) financial security to a retiree.

C) it to a retiree.

D) it to him or her.

CONTINUE

Fully aware of such financial insecurities, many older workers who might have retired had their savings been larger have [37] <u>chosed</u> to stay in the workforce. Their motives are understandable, but their actions have nonetheless been met with criticism. Older people who continue working well into their 70s and 80s are often blamed for "holding back" their younger counterparts. This critique has been directed in particular at specialized sectors of the economy, such as academia, that [38] <u>have their chips</u> on highly-skilled workers and that offer relatively few full-time positions.

CONTINUE

37

A) NO CHANGE
B) chose
C) chosen
D) choosed

38

A) NO CHANGE
B) are all-in
C) rely
D) sit

Test 3

The situation among full-time professors helps to illustrate the concerns and complaints that younger workers might have. At present, the average age for a full-time professor in the United States is 55, although professors who earn top administrative positions **[39]** and high salaries, $125,000 or more) can be in their 60s or 70s at the highest-ranked institutions.

[40] Likewise, rewarding older professionals in this manner is not always the best way to cultivate the skills that the profession itself requires. **[41]** Younger professors are often fluent in the use of online Learning Management Systems and other supremely useful classroom technologies. By rewarding older professors who do not possess technology aptitudes, colleges may in fact do a disservice to students, and may even discourage talented and innovative workers from pursuing careers in academia.

39

A) NO CHANGE
B) and high salaries ($125,000 or more,
C) and (high salaries, $125,000 or more)
D) and high salaries ($125,000 or more)

40

A) NO CHANGE
B) Consequently,
C) Surprisingly,
D) Unfortunately,

41

Which choice would most effectively support the writer's argument at this point in the paragraph?

A) NO CHANGE
B) Students often have an easier time relating to younger professors, many of whom excel in explaining "difficult" topics in terms of students' cultural and career interests.
C) Older professors may possess a wealth of obscure knowledge that is useful in specialized research, but often struggle to clearly communicate such knowledge to students.
D) As technology becomes more integrated into classroom experiences, pre-recorded lectures and "adaptive learning" technologies may make some of the more predictable duties of professors unnecessary.

CONTINUE

[1] An awareness of such dilemmas is nonetheless a valuable first step towards finding solutions. [2] Alerted to their own liabilities, [42] todays older workers would do well to focus more intensely on financial literacy and to develop more orderly savings plans. [3] Younger [43] workers for their part, do not need to feel oppressed by an aging job market. [4] While finding new ways to adapt, they can benefit from the experience and wisdom of older professionals. [5] Moreover, these young employees can use their familiarity with technology to build more efficient and harmonious workplace communities. [44]

42

A) NO CHANGE
B) today's older workers'
C) todays' older workers'
D) today's older workers

43

A) NO CHANGE
B) workers, for their part do not need,
C) workers for their part, do not need,
D) workers, for their part, do not need

44

The writer would like to add the following sentence to the paragraph.

> A senior professor, for instance, can guide younger colleagues through the subtleties of long-term research.

The most logical and appropriate placement for this new content would be after

A) sentence 2.
B) sentence 3.
C) sentence 4.
D) sentence 5.

STOP

**If you finish before time is called, you may check your work on this section only.
Do not turn to any other section.**

CONTINUE

Answer Key: Test 3

Passage 1		Passage 2		Passage 3		Passage 4	
1.	B	12.	C	23.	D	34.	B
2.	A	13.	D	24.	C	35.	C
3.	D	14.	C	25.	D	36.	B
4.	C	15.	B	26.	A	37.	C
5.	D	16.	D	27.	C	38.	C
6.	C	17.	D	28.	B	39.	D
7.	B	18.	D	29.	B	40.	D
8.	C	19.	B	30.	B	41.	A
9.	A	20.	A	31.	C	42.	D
10.	C	21.	B	32.	D	43.	D
11.	C	22.	C	33.	D	44.	C

Topic Areas by Question

Expression of Ideas

Passage 1: Questions 3-4, 7-9, 11

Passage 2: Questions 12, 14-16, 18, 21

Passage 3, Questions 24, 26-28, 31, 33

Passage 4, Questions 34, 36, 38, 40-41, 44

Standard English Conventions

Passage 1: Questions 1-2, 5-6, 10

Passage 2: Questions 13, 17, 19-20, 22

Passage 3, Questions 23, 25, 29-30, 32

Passage 4, Questions 35, 37, 39, 42-43

Answer Explanations
Test 3, Pages 54-69

Passage 1, Pages 54-57

1. <u>B</u> is the correct answer.

The underlined portion should indicate who was "performing experiments," Mendel (he) himself. Choose B as the answer that properly places a reference to Mendel after the modifier that begins the sentence. A (discovery), C (basis), and D (genetic inheritance) all create misplaced modifiers that illogically indicate that things or ideas other than Mendel were performing experiments.

2. <u>A</u> is the correct answer.

When used to introduce a clause, "although" should not normally be divided from the clause it introduces with a comma or another unit of punctuation. Thus, choose A and eliminate B and D. C wrongly creates a fragment beginning with "although" after a semicolon.

3. <u>D</u> is the correct answer.

The sentence that contains the underlined portion discusses two specific "versions" of a quality, "seed color," mentioned in the previous sentence. It thus provides an example of a more general idea, so that D is the best choice. A and B both indicate relationships involving reversals, while C indicates a relationship in time, NOT an example that is more specific and simply explains a simultaneous, broad idea.

4. <u>C</u> is the correct answer.

The previous segment of the sentence, and the related sentence about pea color that occurs immediately before, both indicate clear either/or options. C thus is the best indication that the options are absolute and clearly different. A and B both wrongly shift focus to Mendel's process of inquiry (away from his findings about final traits), while D wrongly emphasizes current ideas (not Mendel's ideas).

5. <u>D</u> is the correct answer.

The underlined verb should describe a hypothetical situation, since the Blending Inheritance theory was NOT correct. Use the subjunctive ("were correct . . . would result") for hypothetical conditions and choose D. A is a simple past tense while B and C are present, and these tenses are only appropriate for ACTUAL events.

6. <u>C</u> is the correct answer.

The paragraph describes what Mendel, a researcher from earlier times, did in the past. C, which reflects this situation and is in agreement with verbs in the next sentence such as "inherited" and "reasoned," is the best choice. A indicates past action that continues into the present (and is illogical since Mendel is no longer alive), B is present tense, and D creates a fragment.

7. <u>B</u> is the correct answer.

The sentence that follows the underlined sentence references a "dominant allele," so that the underlined sentence sets up this important finding by presenting Mendel's own term. Choose B and eliminate A, since the term "dominance" itself (as opposed to the ideas behind it) does not appear prominently in later paragraphs. Although the term disappears, how alleles work continues to be an important topic for the passage, so that C and D both use faulty logic in arguing that the information can be eliminated.

8. <u>C</u> is the correct answer.

The sentence that contains the underlined portion already indicates that the plants are either green or yellow. Eliminate A for redundancy and B as a more wordy version of the same information presented in C, but be careful not to choose D ("those of them") which uses vague pronoun references. C is the superior answer because it clearly indicates that the "generation" of plants is Mendel's main interest.

9. <u>A</u> is the correct answer.

According to the passage, the presence of a Y allele will cause peas to be yellow, so that peas without this allele will be green. The sentences should be combined to show that the absence of the Y allele caused the color outcome: A is thus the best choice. B indicates contrast, C reverses the cause-and-effect logic (wrongly indicating that the color CAUSED the absence of the allele), and D indicates a later event, not a reason.

10. <u>C</u> is the correct answer.

The sentence compares the inheritance patterns of humans to the inheritance patterns of, or "those" of, pea plants. C compares the correct items, while A and B both compare inheritance patterns to pea plants and D compares inheritance patterns to complexity, NOT to other inheritance patterns as needed.

11. <u>C</u> is the correct answer.

The underlined portion must provide a direct and logical explanation for the influence of Mendel's research (which mostly concerns peas) on the study of human inheritance. Similar inheritance principles or "underpinnings" in these organisms would form an appropriate connection. Choose C and eliminate A, B, and D, which all concern Mendel's reputation as opposed to how, in his conception, inheritance operates.

Passage 2, Pages 58-61

12. <u>C</u> is the correct answer.

The proposed sentence shifts too much emphasis away from the passage's main topics (the roles and functions of lighthouses) to consider the perspective of "sailors and mariners." Choose C as the most appropriate option, and eliminate A and B, since the proposed sentence discusses emotions ("reassurance") instead of practical reasoning. D does not properly characterize the sentence, which uses an accessible style and only one arguably difficult word ("mariners") that is nonetheless clear as a synonym for "sailors" in context.

13. <u>D</u> is the correct answer.

In this question, eliminate redundant content. That lighthouses operate (or function), that they are indicators (or signals), and that they "long" (or "over time") function are all facts that become evident from other content. Thus, avoid A, B, and C (respectively) and choose D as a concise, effective option.

14. <u>C</u> is the correct answer.

The underlined content should describe the development of technology over "several decades": the term "impressive pace" in C would properly indicate rapid development. A introduces a negative, "fearsome," that is more appropriate for describing emotion. B would better describe an exchange and is too colloquial, while D indicates size, not a process of development over time.

15. <u>B</u> is the correct answer.

The maximum number of lighthouses in use for ANY year, according to the dashed line in the graph, was just over 800 in the mid 1800s. Choose B and eliminate A, which understates the maximum by roughly 400 lighthouses. C and D can both be eliminated because, by the late 1900s, only a small minority of lighthouses and well under 200 were working at any one time

16. <u>D</u> is the correct answer.

The tables indicate that Michigan had the most lighthouses of any state in 1974 but NOT in 1994. D properly reflects this information while A and C are unsubstantiated since only two years specific to Michigan (NOT all the years in a 20-year period for Michigan) are given. B is contradicted by the graph: Michigan had 140 lighthouses in use in 1974, but just under 1200 were in use throughout the country, so that "all other states combined" clearly possessed MORE lighthouses than Michigan did.

17. <u>D</u> is the correct answer.

The sentence should describe HOW lighthouses are built of various materials: "typically built" is a concise and effective phrasing that properly modifies a participle with an adverb. Choose D and eliminate A and C (both of which include the nonexistent word "builtly"). B wrongly describes the lighthouses as "typical" and does so in a manner that wrongly compares lighthouses to materials, and should thus be eliminated.

18. <u>D</u> is the correct answer.

The writer needs to logically explain why lighthouses have "fallen into disuse." More modern navigation systems would logically make old-fashioned lighthouses unnecessary, so choose D. A is a trap answer, since it introduces a negative factor ("seldom constructed to endure") that is CONTRADICTED by the idea in the previous paragraph that lighthouses were built of "strong materials." B (governments) and C (tourists) both shift to new topics that are at best loosely related to the practical need for lighthouses.

19. <u>B</u> is the correct answer.

The underlined sentence should continue the idiom "available to" to identify another group that can access lighthouses. Only B both preserves the idiom and properly creates parallel structure with "to," so that A, C, and D can be readily eliminated.

20. <u>A</u> is the correct answer.

A semicolon should always be followed by a full independent clause, as in A with the clause "one . . . is." Choose this answer and eliminate B (which wrongly treats the subject "one" as plural or confuses it with the object of a preposition "groups"). C and D both create sentence fragments.

21. <u>B</u> is the correct answer.

In the sentence that contains the underlined portion, eliminate redundant content. The history of the United States is naturally "national" (A), an element is an "aspect" (C), and history by definition happens "over time" (D). Only B effectively avoids redundancies of this sort.

22. <u>C</u> is the correct answer.

The sentence that contains the underlined portion should exhibit parallel structure using three verbs: "learn . . . enter . . . climb." Only C creates a proper three-item series with two commas and a final "and". A and B insert unneeded phrases ("and they") while D wrongly inserts a noun ("lighthouses") into the required series of verbs.

Passage 3, Pages 62-65

23. <u>D</u> is the correct answer.

The subject-verb combination "Nobel Foundation . . . commended" should normally be divided only by a non-essential phrase set off by TWO units of punctuation. D (two commas) properly adheres to this convention, while A, B, and C all wrongly use only a single comma.

24. <u>C</u> is the correct answer.

The sentence shifts from a positive idea ("succeed") to a seemingly negative one ("disorienting") and this introduces a contrast. C establishes the only appropriate sentence relationship. A (similar and comparable alternatives), B (direction or extent), and D (similarity) do not fit the sentence's content.

25. <u>D</u> is the correct answer.

The underlined portion of the sentence should feature a pronoun reference to single "newcomer" to Kawabata's writing. Choose D as the correct option for a reference to a single person. A and B are plural while C is only appropriate to non-human things.

26. <u>A</u> is the correct answer.

The underlined portion should describe Shimamura, who makes "excursions" to the resort. To "frequent" an area is to reside in it for a time. A is thus appropriate. B describes the act of setting up a location, C would describe how the resort ITSELF welcomes Shimamura, and D is wordy and awkward in construction.

27. <u>C</u> is the correct answer.

As a whole, the passage uses clear yet formal vocabulary to explain Kawabata's descriptions of nature in an often positive manner. C is appropriate to the passage's style and tone. A and D are inappropriately informal, while B ("flagrant" meaning "bold" or "obvious") uses needlessly advanced vocabulary. B and D can also be seen as indicating negative tones and could be eliminated for this reason.

28. <u>B</u> is the correct answer.

Sentence 7 indicates that a Kawabata novel may not appear to be a fully developed narrative, a point that sentence 1 continues by offering details about the experience of reading Kawabata. Choose B and eliminate A, since the broad sentence 7 should INTRODUCE the details of the paragraph rather than referencing them in a distracting manner at the paragraph's end. C and D both break up analysis of specific Kawabata novels with a very general statement that should preface such analysis instead, and should thus be eliminated.

29. B is the correct answer.

The underlined portion should be in parallel with "To see" earlier in the sentence. Choose B, "to miss," and eliminate A, C, and D as automatically breaking parallelism.

30. B is the correct answer.

The underlined verb should take the subject "plots" by inverted subject-verb agreement. Choose B, and eliminate A and C as wrongly singular. D, "being," would create a fragment after a semicolon and should be eliminated for this reason.

31. C is the correct answer.

The passage indicated earlier on that Shingo is a disappointed character who nonetheless does not change his life. C returns to these themes while supporting the idea that Kawabata's novels urge readers to contemplate. Trap answer A raises a point (parallels between Kawabata himself and Shingo) that the passage does not substantiate in any of its given content. Eliminate this answer, and eliminate B and D as answers that do not directly mention Shingo and thus do not fit the prompt.

32. D is the correct answer.

Kawabata's short "narratives" are the "palm-of-the-hand" stories, and a colon can be used to present a reference to an item in the manner of D. Choose this answer and eliminate A (sentence fragment) and B (absence of punctuation, in which ideas run together). Do not choose trap answer C. Although a colon can set up a phrase or a fragment, a semicolon MUST be followed by an independent clause.

33. D is the correct answer.

Throughout the passage, the writer calls attention to the importance of Kawabata's writing in depicting Japan, and underscores the fact that Kawabata's writings lead readers to contemplate. These themes support D. A ("destined to be forgotten") is overly critical of Kawabata's achievement, while B (childhood) and C (other novelists) raise new topics that are not investigated elsewhere and thus are not effective as concluding statements that return to earlier analysis.

Passage 4, Pages 66-69

34. B is the correct answer.

The paragraph as a whole discusses the various and current difficulties that face older workers, a group that would include the "most experienced employees" mentioned in B. Choose this answer and eliminate A (which emphasizes younger employees), C (which calls attention to a sociological debate), and D (which refers to historical trends). These issues all draw attention away from the older workers and the practical details of their present-day problems.

35. C is the correct answer.

The word "however" should be offset using two commas (according to convention) when it appears in the middle of an independent clause. Choose C and eliminate A and B, since both of these answers wrongly split the subject-verb combination "Maintaining . . . may be" with a semicolon. D wrongly disrupts the same subject-verb combination with a single comma.

36. B is the correct answer.

By definition, a retiree is a person who is no longer employed. Eliminate A as redundant, but be careful of the ambiguous "it" in C and D. This pronoun SHOULD refer to a quality or benefit such as "financial security," so eliminate these answers and choose the much clearer B.

37. C is the correct answer.

When used with an auxiliary verb such as "have" as part of a past tense, "to choose" becomes "chosen." C properly utilizes the phrasing "have chosen." B is the simple past "chose," which cannot appear with auxiliary verbs, while A and D are nonexistent.

38. C is the correct answer.

The underlined portion should explain how specialized economic sectors such as academia respond to "highly-skilled workers." Such sectors would naturally depend on or "rely" on skilled employees. Choose C, and eliminate both A and B as too colloquial or informal. D best describes a physical action and thus does not fit the context.

39. D is the correct answer.

When using parentheses, always use one parenthesis to open the parenthetical phrase and one to close it off. Only ONE parenthesis appears in A, and the same error occurs in B. Make sure also that the parenthetical phrase can be deleted from the sentence without disrupting meaning or grammar. The parenthetical phrase in C would create the faulty parallelism "administrative positions . . . and can be," while D features effective parallelism with the paired-off noun phrases "administrative positions . . . high salaries" when the parenthetical phrase in this answer is deleted.

40. D is the correct answer.

The previous sentence indicates that older professors have notable administrative and salary benefits, while the sentence that contains the underlined portions critiques such rewards. D properly indicates the shift to a negative tone. A (similarity), B (cause and effect), and C (unexpected information, with a faulty assumption about the reader's own knowledge) do not properly register the movement from a positive (reward) to a negative (drawback) topic.

41. <u>A</u> is the correct answer.

In the paragraph, the writer calls attention to the drawbacks faced by "older professionals" and to the "technology aptitudes" of younger professors. Calling attention to the technology abilities of "Younger professors" in A would effectively support the writer's discussion. B and C both raise a possible advantage of younger professors (communication) but NOT one related to the writer's existing argument about technology. D raises the topic of technology but does NOT draw a direct link to professors based on age group.

42. <u>D</u> is the correct answer.

In the underlined phrase, "today" should be a possessive (since the workers belong to the current time) and "worker" should be a plural noun that takes the verb "would do well." Choose D, eliminate A for presenting the plural noun "todays," and eliminate B and C for presenting the plural possessive "workers'."

43. <u>D</u> is the correct answer.

At the underlined portion, the subject-verb phrase "workers . . . do not need" should not be separated by a single comma (eliminating A and B). The idiomatic phrase "need to" should also not be split by a comma (eliminating B and C). D thus features the correct punctuation and properly offsets the non-essential phrase "for their part" with two commas.

44. <u>C</u> is the correct answer.

The proposed sentence offers an example of cooperation between older and younger workers, a "benefit" that is directly mentioned in sentence 4. Choose C as the position that allows the sentence to function as a continuation of a topic. A mentions older workers only, while B and D focus entirely on younger workers; NONE of these choices directly present the topic of collaboration between older and younger workers in a manner that would effectively introduce the example in the new sentence.

Test 4

Writing and Language
2018 SAT Practice

Writing and Language Test

35 MINUTES, 44 QUESTIONS

Turn to Section 2 of your answer sheet to answer the questions in this section.

Each passage below is accompanied by a number of questions. For some questions, you will consider how the passage might be revised to improve the expression of ideas. For other questions, you will consider how the passage might be edited to correct errors in sentence structure, usage, or punctuation. A passage or a question may be accompanied by one or more graphics (such as a table or graph) that you will consider as you make revising and editing decisions.

Some questions will direct you to an underlined portion of a passage. Other questions will direct you to a location in a passage or ask you to think about the passage as a whole.

After reading each passage, choose the answer to each question that most effectively improves the quality of writing in the passage or that makes the passage conform to the conventions of standard written English. Many questions will include a "NO CHANGE" option. Choose that option if you think the best choice is to leave the relevant portion of the passage as it is.

Questions 1-11 are based on the following passage.

Photographing Asia: The Work of Linnaeus Tripe

[1] As both a traveler and a photographer, Captain Linnaeus Tripe had the gift of being in the right place at the right time. [2] His career behind the camera began in the early 1850s, when he became one of the founding members of the Photographic Society in London. [3] **1** Until then, the activity that he is remembered

1
A) NO CHANGE
B) As a result,
C) Indeed,
D) However,

for took him well beyond the British metropolis and into the inner reaches of India and Myanmar (formerly Burma). [4] On his travels through Asia, Tripe took thousands of photographs of temples, pagodas, and carvings. [5] Yet in its own right, each visual is an indication **2** to Tripe's prowess in photographic composition. [6] Clear of contour, deep of perspective, Tripe's images are lucid records of landmarks and landscapes. [7] These photographs are rich in atmosphere: his open skies and scintillating foliage suggest a world of profound calm. **3**

2

A) NO CHANGE
B) of
C) for
D) that

3

The writer wishes to add the following sentence to the paragraph.

> When considered alongside one another, these photographs constitute a precise portrait of Myanmar's culture.

The best placement for this new content would be after

A) sentence 1.
B) sentence 3.
C) sentence 4.
D) sentence 7.

CONTINUE

Tripe's photographic travels, which [4] preceded under the auspices of the East India Company, were cut short in 1860 as the result of budgetary problems. [5] Recently, viewers far from Myanmar were given a chance to appreciate Tripe's talents. By gathering roughly sixty of his images into a few spacious galleries, New York City's Metropolitan Museum of Art created an affecting showcase. Titled *Captain Linnaeus Tripe: Photographer of India and Burma,* [6] new questions about Tripe' accomplishments were encouraged by the exhibition. Did he simply have the luck to capture a few stunning sights? [7] Whatever explanation for Tripe's accomplishment ultimately emerges, there is no question that his work attests to the quiet power of photography.

4

A) NO CHANGE
B) preceeded
C) proceeded
D) proceded

5

The writer is considering deleting the underlined portion. Should the sentence be kept or deleted?

A) Kept, because it provides an effective transition.
B) Kept, because it explains Tripe's current fame.
C) Deleted, because the possible viewers are not designated in the passage.
D) Deleted, because it is critical of Tripe's legacy.

6

A) NO CHANGE
B) the exhibition encouraged new questions about Tripe's accomplishments.
C) Tripe's accomplishments were questioned anew by the exhibition.
D) what Tripe accomplished was questioned anew by the exhibition.

7

Which choice most logically provides another, related question that the showcase would inspire?

A) Or was he better-trained than is often assumed?
B) Or did he excel regardless of his chosen subject?
C) Or has his achievement been obscured until now?
D) Or did he pursue innovation in a manner that his contemporaries could not understand?

CONTINUE

The show's initial galleries featured a sampling of Tripe's nautical and military images from Devonport, England. These works are conscientious and clear in execution; in their incorporation of overriding pattern and aerial perspective, **[8]** from time to time Tripe's shots are occasionally inspired. However, they don't entirely prepare viewers for the vacated vistas and brutal symmetries of Tripe's Asian explorations. Intricately carved arcades, scalloped rock faces, and palm trees that seem to rise gingerly into the air **[9]** is among the sights Tripe captured.

8

A) NO CHANGE
B) Tripe's shots of features of Devonport are
C) Tripe's shots are
D) DELETE the underlined portion.

9

A) NO CHANGE
B) has been
C) was
D) are

On the basis of such evidence, the sights of India and Burma unleashed Tripe's powers of resourcefulness, though technical necessities also shaped his craft. Because glass negatives were poorly adapted to the humidity of Southeast Asia, Tripe produced his images using gold-toned paper negatives. **10** It imparted an ethereal, lithograph-like effect to much of Tripe's output. He also developed ingenious perceptual effects. To capture the inscriptions of the Brihadishvara Temple in southern India in their entirety, Tripe combined photograph upon photograph to generate a 360-degree continuous panorama. The civilizations Tripe documented are rich in centuries-old architectural wonders, **11** but he photographed them in a spirit of innovation.

10

A) NO CHANGE

B) That imparted

C) The country imparted

D) This process imparted

11

Which choice best concludes the passage by summarizing one of the writer's important points about Tripe's photographic practices?

A) NO CHANGE

B) but they made Tripe the preeminent photographer of his generation.

C) and are even more respected today thanks to Tripe's endeavors.

D) and have continued to intrigue the photographers who sought them out long after Tripe did.

CONTINUE

Questions 12-22 are based on the following passage and supplementary material.

A Home Turf for TIRF Microscopy

Scientists at the National Institute of Biomedical Imaging and Bioengineering (NIBIB) have combined two different microscope technologies [12] to create sharper images of rapidly moving processes inside a cell. In a paper published today in Nature Methods, Hari Shroff, Ph.D., chief of NIBIB's lab section on High Resolution Optical Imaging (HROI), describes his new improvements to traditional Total Internal Reflection Fluorescence (TIRF) microscopy. TIRF microscopy [13] eliminates the sample at a sharp angle so that the light reflects back, making visible only a thin section of the sample that is extremely close to the coverslip. This innovative process creates very high contrast images because it eliminates [14] much to the background out-of-focus light that [15] tried and true microscopes pick up.

See Page 106 for the citation for this text.

12

The writer wishes to indicate that the NIBIB team has engineered an improved technology with at least one well-defined application to the study of biology. Which choice accomplishes this goal?

A) NO CHANGE

B) to reduce the energy input required for high-intensity microscope imaging.

C) to radically redefine how microscope-oriented investigations are conducted.

D) to increase image resolution to such a point that formerly "undetectable" forms are visible.

13

A) NO CHANGE

B) illustrates

C) illuminates

D) explicates

14

A) NO CHANGE

B) much of

C) many to

D) many of

15

A) NO CHANGE

B) conventional

C) everybody's normal

D) humdrum

CONTINUE

While TIRF microscopy has been used in cell biology for decades, it <u>16 produces: blurry images, of small features,</u> within cells. In the past, super-resolution microscopy techniques applied to TIRF microscopes have been able <u>17 to improve the resolution, and such attempts occasionally result in higher speeds.</u> As a result, many cellular processes remain too small or fast to observe.

16

A) NO CHANGE

B) produces: blurry images of small features

C) produces blurry images, of small features,

D) produces blurry images of small features

17

Which choice best reflects the information in the graph below?

A) NO CHANGE

B) improve the resolution, but such attempts always compromise speed.

C) improve the resolution, since such attempts have little effect on speed.

D) improve the resolution, although there is little correlation between resolution and speed.

Five Configurations of a TIRF Microscope (developed 2011, deployed 2013-2015)

Measurement Scale: 0 (weakest) to 100 (optimal)

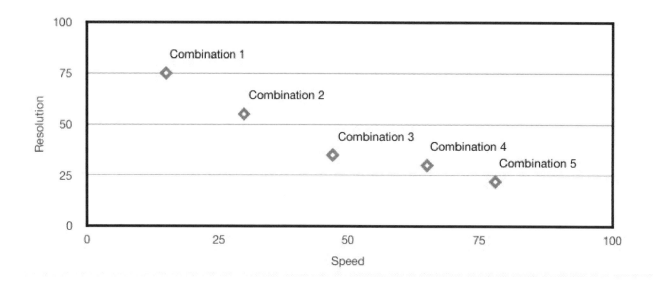

CONTINUE ➤

Shroff and his team realized that if they could take a high-speed, super-resolution microscope and modify it to act like a TIRF microscope, they could obtain the benefits of both. Instant structured illumination microscopy (iSIM), developed by the Shroff lab in 2013, can capture video at 100 frames per second, **18** which is exactly four times faster than a digital camera typically can. However, an iSIM microscope does not have the contrast that TIRF microscopes do. The team designed a simple "mask" that blocked most of the illumination from the iSIM—mimicking a TIRF microscope. Combining the strengths of both types of **19** microscopy, that enabled the researchers to observe rapidly moving objects about 10 times faster than they could with other microscopes at similar resolution.

18

The writer wishes to include accurate and relevant information based on the following chart, which lists the frames per second for various devices.

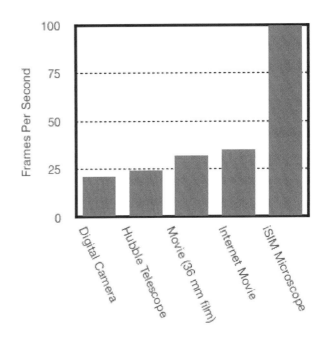

Which choice best accomplishes this goal?

A) NO CHANGE

B) which is almost four times faster than an Internet video recorder typically can.

C) which is roughly three times faster than movie and Internet video recorders typically can.

D) which is exactly four times faster than movie or Internet video recorders typically can.

19

A) NO CHANGE

B) microscopy, it enabled

C) microscopy enabled

D) microscopy enable

CONTINUE

"TIRF microscopy has been around for more than 30 years and it is so useful that it will likely be around for at least the next 30," said Shroff. "Our method improves the spatial resolution of TIRF microscopy without **[20]** compromising speed. This accomplishment is something that no other microscope can do. We hope it helps us clarify high-speed biology that might otherwise be hidden or blurred by other microscopes so that we can better understand how biological processes work."

For example, with the new microscope, Shroff and his team were able to follow rapidly moving Rab11 particles near the plasma membrane of human cells. **[21]** As envisioned by Shroff, such observations represent an improvement over the possibilities of earlier microscopes. Attached to molecular cargo that are transported around the cell, these particles move so fast that they are blurred when imaged by other microscopes. **[22]** They also used their technique to reveal the dynamics and spatial distribution of HRas, a protein that has been implicated in facilitating the growth of cancerous tumors.

20

Which choice best combines the two sentences at the underlined portion

A) compromising speed—accomplishing something

B) compromising speed, and there you have accomplished something

C) compromising speed, because it's accomplishing something

D) compromising speed, when this is accomplished being something

21

The writer is considering deleting the underlined content from the paragraph. Should this sentence be kept or deleted?

A) Kept, because it effectively introduces the topic of how HRas moves through the body.

B) Kept, because it returns to an important point about how the different elements of a cell are arranged.

C) Deleted, because it is not clear exactly which observations the writer is referencing.

D) Deleted, because it does little more than re-state ideas established earlier.

22

A) NO CHANGE

B) They also used there

C) The researchers also used their

D) The researchers also used there

CONTINUE

Questions 23-33 are based on the following passage.

The Challenges and Triumphs of ESL Instruction

English as a Second Language (or ESL) students are commonly identified as people who have considearble English competency. **23** <u>This is a bizarre assumption.</u> People who emigrate to an English speaking country with only the ability to use the language from their home country have great challenges ahead; many of these people are today's ESL students.

Imagine going into a grocery store, doctor's office, or your children's school without recognizing any of the words that are being spoken or written. A beginning ESL student often has to start the language learning experience at a very **24** <u>basic level, often he or she identifies</u> words by looking at pictures, pinpointing colors, and using numbers. Survival skills that include making a personal introduction, relaying a phone number, and knowing when to call an emergency service **25** <u>which are</u> some of the first lessons to be learned.

23

Which choice provides the most appropriate and effective transition?

A) NO CHANGE

B) This is not necessarily the case.

C) This definition remains unclear.

D) This consensus is increasingly popular.

24

A) NO CHANGE

B) basic level, often by identifying

C) basic level, who identifies

D) basic level; identifying

25

A) NO CHANGE

B) that are

C) being

D) are

CONTINUE

Test 4

In terms of English language learning, even a highly educated person may need to make progress slowly and methodically. [26] Often, doing so is difficult for adult learners. These individuals have limited time because of financial and family responsibilities.

ESL programs are accessible throughout the United States free of charge through Literacy Volunteers of America (LVA). These programs are commonly available by county or region. Each individual organization determines [27] its' community's needs and provides programs that can include one-on-one tutoring, group classes, and citizenship training. Programs strive to serve as many people as possible and to accommodate [28] all sorts of kinds of learning. Volunteers who are specially trained to work with students come from all walks of life. These volunteers may include career educators, homemakers, or retired professionals who are willing to commit time to work with students. Volunteers and their students regularly meet in local libraries, [29] where there are space and resources available for tutoring sessions.

26

Which choice most effectively combines the sentences at the underlined portion?

A) Because these individuals are adult learners, doing so is often difficult for them because of

B) Doing so is often difficult for adult learners, who have

C) They are adult learners, and doing so is often difficult as they have

D) Them being adult learners, they often find doing so difficult, having

---

27

A) NO CHANGE

B) it's community needs

C) its community's needs

D) it's communities' needs

28

A) NO CHANGE

B) various levels

C) unpredictable dreams

D) sundry anomalies

29

A) NO CHANGE

B) where there is

C) where there was

D) where

CONTINUE

[1] An ESL instructor has an enormous responsibility to be positive because **30** <u>adult students want</u> to experience a sense of accomplishment and to feel increased self-esteem. [2] Thus, lessons are often customized to include essential skills for an improved personal lifestyle. [3] A parent may have the responsibility of taking children to school or for medical and dental check-ups. [4] Those people who are in the workforce often wish to communicate with co-workers and hope that English lessons may lead to advancement in their profession. [5] Further, it is essential that the teacher strive to understand students' individual needs and create approachable lesson plans. [6] ESL instructors should help their students to set short-term and long-term goals. **31**

30

The writer is considering revising the underlined portion of the paragraph to read as follows

> adult students—much like students at almost any stage of English aptitude—want

Should the writer make this revision?

A) Yes, because it resolves a point of uncertainty that was introduced earlier in the passage.

B) Yes, because it introduces a comparison that the writer examines later in the paragraph.

C) No, because it draws attention away from the paragraph's focus on the training of ESL instructors.

D) No, because it distracts from the paragraph's focus on adult ESL students.

31

To make the order of ideas in the paragraph most logical, sentence 5 should be placed.

A) where it is now.

B) after sentence 1.

C) after sentence 2.

D) after sentence 3.

CONTINUE ➡

Attending classes and completing written homework are fundamental to the success of an ESL student. Conversation skills demand efforts towards everyday practice, especially [32] if a student lives in a home where there are no other residents who speak English. Students should be encouraged to seek opportunities to speak in English in as many contexts as possible, perhaps at stores or with English-speaking friends. It is advisable [33] where instructors will speak only English at the classes, further immersing the students in English. While building such competence may take time, it is also a rewarding experience for student and instructor alike.

32

The writer wishes to call attention to a challenge that some ESL students may face in attaining aptitude in English. Which choice best accomplishes this goal?

A) NO CHANGE

B) if a student attends an ESL program that had been founded in the recent past.

C) if a student's community encourages fluency in languages other than English.

D) if a student's work schedule calls for interaction with a large number of clients or customers.

33

A) NO CHANGE

B) having the instructors speak

C) that instructors speak

D) instructors speaking

CONTINUE

Questions 34-44 are based on the following passage.

Thankful for the Macy's Parade

Towering hot air balloons, marching bands from across America, dancers, floats, and famous entertainers bring massive crowds of people to New York City annually for the Macy's Thanksgiving Day Parade. The parade has become a [34] tremendous hubbub for individuals and families everywhere who often plan their holiday meals around viewing the spectacle. Since 1954, the parade [35] will be televised nationally to the delight of millions of viewers. By the most recent estimates, 3.5 million people typically come to Manhattan to view the parade, with another 5 million people watching it on TV.

34

A) NO CHANGE
B) flattering practice
C) cherished tradition
D) sacred rite

35

A) NO CHANGE
B) could have been
C) has been
D) is

CONTINUE

Test 4

The first Macy's Thanksgiving Day Parade was held [36] during a prosperous era in American history, the Roaring Twenties. In 1924, Macy's planned the parade during the busy holiday season to celebrate the opening of the department store's flagship at 34th Street and 7th Avenue in New York City. The "World's Largest Store" had a million square feet of retail space and encompassed a full city block, [37] although the modern definition of a city "block" as 100,000 square feet was not fully applicable then. The premiere parade had attractions that complemented the Mother Goose nursery rhyme theme of the store's holiday windows. [38] Visitors flocked to the central parade location, often by riding to Midtown on the city's rapidly-growing subway system. The highlight of the parade was the final attraction, the arrival of Santa Claus.

36

A) NO CHANGE
B) with
C) of
D) at

37

The writer is considering deleting the underlined portion and ending the sentence with a period after "block." Should the underlined content be kept or deleted in this manner?

A) Kept, because it resolves a point of uncertainty that emerged in a previous paragraph.
B) Kept, because it helps the reader to understand why coordinating the Parade is so difficult.
C) Deleted, because it introduces a fact that is completely unrelated to the content of the passage.
D) Deleted, because it distracts from the discussion of the Parade's history and arrangement.

38

The writer wishes to indicate that the Thanksgiving Day Parade involved cooperation between different businesses or institutions in New York City. Which choice best accomplishes this goal?

A) NO CHANGE
B) Among those who take the greatest pride in the Parade are the Macy's employees who volunteer their time and energy.
C) At the first downtown Parade, there were even animals on loan from the city's nearby Central Park Zoo.
D) City officials appreciated the cheerful and age-inclusive nature of the showcase as a whole.

CONTINUE

[1] Much has changed since Macy's hosted its first Thanksgiving Day Parade. [2] At present, the thrilling features include the massive hot air **39** balloons that are inflated to large sizes in Central Park the day before the parade. [3] It takes 90 people to guide each of the balloons through the streets. [4] Each of the giant balloons utilizes between 300,000 and 700,000 cubic feet of helium at a minimum cost of $510,000 for each balloon. [5] Each year, some of the balloons that are brought to the parade represent popular animated figures. [6] Among the classic characters **40** is Charlie Brown and The Grinch. [7] Some of the most recent additions include beloved 21st-century Disney characters, such as Olaf from the animated feature *Frozen*. [8] Many of the balloon handlers are Macy's employees from the Northeast who are given the opportunity to participate. **41**

39

A) NO CHANGE

B) balloons that are inflated, or filled with gas,

C) balloons that are inflated in Central Park

D) balloons that are situated in Central Park and inflated there

40

A) NO CHANGE

B) was

C) has been

D) are

41

To make the order of ideas in the paragraph most logical, sentence 8 should be placed

A) where it is now.

B) after sentence 1.

C) after sentence 3.

D) after sentence 5.

CONTINUE

Test 4

Floats have long been an exciting attraction in the parade and are often themed for current Broadway musicals; they can also represent **42** a variety of beloved figures from popular films or cartoons. Designed to be elaborate and colorful, **43** Moonachie, New Jersey, is where these floats are constructed in the Macy's parade studio with materials like wood, fiberglass, metal and foam. The studio is a huge warehouse where the new balloons are also made and tested for durability.

There are some true similarities between the parade that first occurred nearly a century ago and today's version. The parade remains a festive, imaginative celebration that ushers in the holiday retail season. It **44** continues to thrill observers and still to conclude right in front of the Macy's flagship store on 34th Street, with the final attraction still being the arrival of Santa Claus to usher in holiday joy.

42

The writer wishes to introduce information indicating that the parade spectacles can serve a purpose that has not yet been mentioned for any element of the parade. Which choice best accomplishes this goal?

A) NO CHANGE

B) commercial entities like Delta Airlines and Entenmann's Cakes.

C) various moments that are related to the performing arts.

D) characters that have come to be regarded as classic.

43

A) NO CHANGE

B) where these floats are constructed is Moonachie, New Jersey, in the Macy's parade studio

C) the Macy's parade studio in Moonachie, New Jersey, is where these floats are constructed

D) these floats are constructed in the Macy's parade studio in Moonachie, New Jersey,

44

A) NO CHANGE

B) it continues thrilling observers to it and still to it concluding right in front

C) it continues to thrill observers and to it still concludes right in front

D) it continues to thrill observers and still concludes right in front

STOP

If you finish before time is called, you may check your work on this section only.
Do not turn to any other section.

Answer Key on the Next Page

Answer Key: Test 4

Passage 1		Passage 2		Passage 3		Passage 4	
1.	D	12.	A	23.	B	34.	C
2.	B	13.	C	24.	B	35.	C
3.	C	14.	B	25.	D	36.	A
4.	C	15.	B	26.	B	37.	D
5.	A	16.	D	27.	C	38.	C
6.	B	17.	B	28.	B	39.	C
7.	B	18.	C	29.	A	40.	D
8.	C	19.	C	30.	D	41.	C
9.	D	20.	A	31.	B	42.	B
10.	D	21.	D	32.	A	43.	D
11.	A	22.	C	33.	C	44.	D

Topic Areas by Question

Expression of Ideas

Passage 1: Questions 1, 3, 5, 7-8, 11

Passage 2: Questions 12, 15, 17-18, 20-21

Passage 3, Questions 23, 25, 28, 30-32

Passage 4, Questions 34, 37-39, 41-42

Standard English Conventions

Passage 1: Questions 2, 4, 6, 9-10

Passage 2: Questions 13-14, 16, 19, 22

Passage 3, Questions 24-25, 27, 29, 33

Passage 4, Questions 35-36, 40, 43-44

Answer Explanations
Test 4, Pages 80-96

Passage 1, Pages 80-84

1. D is the correct answer.

The sentence that contains the underlined portion follows a description of Tripe's activities in London, and indicates that he is remembered for work that took place beyond the "British metropolis" (London). D best calls attention to the shift in topic and to the contrast of locations. A indicates conditions in time (and wrongly implies that Tripe, who is dead, will be active at some later point), B indicates a cause-and-effect relationship, and C indicates similar, intensified ideas.

2. B is the correct answer.

The proper idiomatic phrase for "indication" is "indication of" for items (such as visuals) that serve as demonstrations or evidence. Choose B and eliminate A and C as breaking the idiom. D, "indication that," is idiomatically correct when introducing a full clause, yet does NOT do so here and should be eliminated.

3. C is the correct answer.

The new sentence describes "these photographs," which depict Asian culture and which are introduced in sentence 4. Choose C as involving the best placement. A would place the description of the photographs before an effective explanation of Tripe's travels through Asia, while B places the new sentence after sentence 3 (which does not directly mention "photographs" and thus makes the "these photographs" reference problematic). D is a trap answer: the proposed sentence discusses depictions of "culture" in Tripe's photography, yet sentence 7 only describes natural sights, so that the new sentence does not logically continue the same topic.

4. <u>C</u> is the correct answer.

The correct diction choice would explain how Tripe's career happened, moved along, or "proceeded" over time. Choose C and eliminate A (a form of "preceded," which means "to go before"). Both B and D are misspellings or nonexistent forms.

5. <u>A</u> is the correct answer.

With the underlined sentence, the writer references viewers "far from Myanmar," who might (on the basis of the next sentence) see the Tripe exhibition in New York. The underlined content is thus an effective transition as noted in A. However, in gesturing towards the topic of the exhibition and noting Tripe's "talents," the underlined sentence does not explain WHY Tripe is famous (eliminating B), explain who exactly the "viewers" are just yet (eliminating C), or offer a criticism of Tripe's work (eliminating D).

6. <u>B</u> is the correct answer.

The underlined portion should refer to something that could be "Titled," such as the Tripe "exhibition." Choose B to avoid a misplaced modifier, since the other choices wrongly and illogically indicate that questions (A), accomplishments (C), and what Tripe accomplished (D) take formal titles.

7. <u>B</u> is the correct answer.

The previous question is about the content of Tripe's photographs and indicates that he was simply lucky; the following question ("Or") should provide an alternative that is also about the same topic. B indicates that tripe was not limited by the "subjects" of his photographs and is an effective answer. A (training) focuses on a different topic, C shifts emphasis away from Tripe's specific photographs to his broader reputation, and D (contemporaries) also introduces a fundamentally different topic.

8. <u>C</u> is the correct answer.

This question involves redundant content. The phrase "from time to time" is an unnecessary re-wording of "occasionally" (eliminating A) and the context of the paragraph makes it clear that Tripe's shots were "of features of Devonport" (eliminating B). D, however, would result in a fragment after a semicolon, so that C is the best answer.

9. <u>D</u> is the correct answer.

The subject of the sentence consists of nouns joined by "and" ("arcades . . . faces . . . trees") and is thus plural. Choose D and eliminate A, B, and C, all of which are singular.

10. <u>D</u> is the correct answer.

The underlined portion should describe what, exactly, "imparted" specific qualities to Tripe's photographs. Naturally, the "process" of their creation would be responsible for their qualities. Choose D, and eliminate A and B (which have ambiguous pronouns that could refer to "humidity," "Southeast Asia," or some other undefined item). C is problematic because it is not clear from the reference which country (India or Burma) would impart the effects.

11. <u>A</u> is the correct answer.

The paragraph indicates that Tripe used "ingenious perceptual effects," which would naturally indicate a "spirit of innovation" in his photography. Choose A, and eliminate B and C (which are about Tripe's reputation, not his "photographic practices" as demanded by the prompt). D wrongly shifts too much focus away from Tripe and onto later photographers.

Passage 2, Pages 85-88

12. <u>A</u> is the correct answer.

According to the question prompt, the underlined portion should relate directly to the study of biology. A, which mentions "processes inside a cell," fulfills this condition. B (energy use), C (new terms of investigation), and D (resolution) all indicate possible improvements to microscope examinations, but do NOT reference biological study in any clear way.

13. <u>C</u> is the correct answer.

In context, the sample described in the sentence would reflect back light. C properly refers to the context of light transmission involving the sample. A would indicate that the sample is being removed, while B and D would both indicate that the example is being explained, NOT that there is light transmission involved.

14. <u>B</u> is the correct answer.

The underlined portion refers to "light," which can be measured but not (like words that take "many") counted in any logical way. This guideline eliminates C and D, while the correct idiomatic phrase for a portion of light is "much of" the light. Thus, eliminate A and choose B as the best answer.

15. <u>B</u> is the correct answer.

The "microscopes" described by the underlined portion should be contrasted with the "innovative" microscopes mentioned earlier. B, "conventional," offers the proper contrast. A is needlessly informal, as is C (which introduces a distracting reference to "everybody"). D, "humdrum," means "dull" and is thus too negative.

16. <u>D</u> is the correct answer.

The phrase indicating what the microscopy "produces" is a single, concise, and connected idea that should not be split by punctuation. Eliminate A and B, then consider that the SPECIFIC content of the images is an essential detail of the sentence and should NOT be offset by commas as in C. D is thus the best choice because it does not disrupt closely-connected thoughts.

17. <u>B</u> is the correct answer.

According to the graph, there is a strong inverse correlation between resolution and speed, since improved resolution is linked to lower speeds. Choose B on the basis of this reading. A wrongly indicates that speed and resolution improve in tandem, C wrongly indicates that the speeds stay constant, and D wrongly indicates that there is not a general relationship between the qualities.

18. <u>C</u> is the correct answer.

In the chart, both 36 mm movies and Internet movies register at over 25 but less than 37.5 (halfway between 25 and 50) frames per second. A good estimate would be one-third of the frames per second of the iSIM microscope. Choose C. A is inaccurate, since a digital camera registers less than 25 frames per second and is not "exactly" one fourth as fast as the iSIM microscope. Both B and D wrongly indicate that the iSIM is faster than an Internet video by a factor of four (NOT three) and should be eliminated for this reason.

19. <u>C</u> is the correct answer.

The verb "enabled" takes the singular subject "Combining" in the main independent clause of the sentence. Choose C, and eliminate A and B as choices that interrupt the subject-verb combination with single commas and unnecessary transitions. D wrongly indicates that "Combining" is plural.

20. <u>A</u> is the correct answer.

The combined version of the sentence should have a concise and logical transition. In A, the dash to offset a longer, somewhat new idea and the word "accomplishing" (which refers back to the "method") create an effective new version. Choose this option and eliminate the wordier, more awkward versions B (which also brings in the unnecessary pronoun "you"), C, and D.

21. <u>D</u> is the correct answer.

In the passage, the previous paragraph clearly explained that Shroff's microscope and its method represent improvements. The underlined sentence repeats this idea without adding meaningful new information. Choose D, but avoid C, since the sentence DOES clearly refer to observations made in the previous sentence. The sentence only describes microscopes and thus does not refer to the protein HRas (eliminating A) or to any other biological information (eliminating B).

22. <u>C</u> is the correct answer.

In the original version, the pronoun "They" is ambiguous and could refer to "particles" or "microscopes" (items that would not develop a research technique). C properly clarifies that "They" should refer to "The researchers" behind a technique that they possessed, or "their" technique. A and B both feature the unclear pronoun "They," while B and D feature "there" (place or situation) instead of "their" (possessive).

Passage 3, Pages 89-92

23. <u>B</u> is the correct answer.

In the paragraph, the writer shifts from the belief that ESL students have "considerable competency" in English to the contrasting idea that ESL students actually have limited English skills and face "great challenges." B properly casts doubt on the sentence that precedes it and sets up a new conception. A is wrongly critical of the paragraph's first sentence (which is a mistaken but not "bizarre" or strongly negative assumption), C wrongly characterizes the first sentence as unclear, and D calls attention to popular perceptions (a subject that does not lead into the final sentence of the paragraph).

24. <u>B</u> is the correct answer.

While A creates a comma splice, B corrects this error by placing the reindependent clause "he or she identifies" with the transitional phrase "by identifying." C wrongly uses "who" (which can only refer to people) to refer to "level," while D places a fragment starting with "identifying" after a semicolon.

25. <u>D</u> is the correct answer.

The main subject-verb combination of the sentence is "skills . . . are". Both A and B insert unnecessary transitional references (and thus turn the sentence into a long fragment), while C ("being") does not feature a verb that creates a main independent clause. Only D contains the correct subject-verb construction.

26. <u>B</u> is the correct answer.

When combining sentences, try for a sentence structure that is effectively concise and well-coordinated. B properly indicates that making progress in learning English ("Doing so") is difficult for "adult learners," who are then properly referenced with the pronoun "who." Choose this answer and eliminate A (with its awkward repetition of "because"), C (with an awkward "and" construction that separates "doing so" from the action that it describes) and D (with its non-grammatical phrase "Them being" and its choppy structure).

27. <u>C</u> is the correct answer.

The underlined portion should refer the needs of an organization's community, or to "its" community's needs. C uses the proper possessive, while A uses a nonexistent form (its') and B and D both wrongly use the contraction of "it is."

28. <u>B</u> is the correct answer.

The underlined portion is part of an analytic discussion of programs that "accommodate" many people from "all walks of life": a large group of this sort would, logically, feature varied skill levels. Choose B and eliminate A as wordy and redundant ("sorts," "kinds"), as well as C as illogical (since the variations in skill have been predicted) and out of context ("dreams" as too emotional). D uses needlessly elevated vocabulary ("sundry" meaning "various," "anomalies" meaning "oddities") and can be eliminated for this reason.

29. <u>A</u> is the correct answer.

The "libraries" should be referred to as a place, "where" the space and resources (plural subject) "are." Choose A. B and C both wrongly use a singular verb, while D wrongly omits a verb altogether.

30. <u>D</u> is the correct answer.

As becomes clear from the paragraph's discussion of students who are also parents or who are in the workforce, the writer's focus here is the topic of adult students. The revision thus distracts from this age group, so choose D. A ("uncertainty," a possibility that never emerges in terms of age groups) misconstrues the informative nature of the passage as a whole. Use the same the same logic that justifies D to eliminate B (which wrongly indicates that the writer returns to younger age groups) and C (since the paragraph focuses on the interaction of adult students and ESL instructors, NOT on the training of instructors).

31. <u>B</u> is the correct answer.

Sentence 5 describes a "Further" important duty of ESL instructors: a similar duty is outlined in sentence 1, while the OUTCOME of such duties is discussed in sentence 2. Choose B and eliminate A, which places sentence 5 after EXAMPLES of duties (sentences 3 and 4) that it should introduce instead. C would illogically place sentence 5 after an outcome ("Thus") of the duties that it describes, while D would break the presentation of examples with a more general statement.

32. <u>A</u> is the correct answer.

One challenge that an ESL student would face is not having opportunities to speak English; such a difficulty would be natural in the "home" described in A. Choose this answer and eliminate B and D, which describe a student's ESL program (B) and activities (D) but not CHALLENGES or possible negatives related to these topics. C is a trap answer: a community that encourages fluency "in languages other than English" may STILL present opportunities to learn English, which it does not clearly exclude from everyday life.

33. <u>C</u> is the correct answer.

The underlined portion should use the proper grammar for a recommendation or a wish that is "advisable": "that instructors speak" is a proper use of the subjunctive for this condition. Choose C, and eliminate A (indicating place). B and D both use awkward -ing forms that do not fit the use of the subjunctive.

Passage 4, Pages 93-96

34. <u>C</u> is the correct answer.

The passage indicates that the Thanksgiving Day Parade is both valued and prioritized: C, "cherished tradition," would properly describe such a long-valued event. A ("hubbub") indicates noise or frantic activity, B ("flattering," often negative) indicates compliments, and D ("sacred") indicates religious devotion. Eliminate these answers as inappropriate to the context.

35. <u>C</u> is the correct answer.

According to the passage, the parade was televised in 1954 and has continued to be televised in the years since. C is the only appropriate answer for action that began in the past and has continued into the present. A indicates the future, B indicates an event that might have happened (but apparently did not), and D only indicates present action, not past-into-present action.

36. <u>A</u> is the correct answer.

The proper idiomatic phrase involving an "era" is "during an era" for actions that take place as the era is underway. Choose A and eliminate B (accompaniment), C (possession), and D (place) as using the wrong idioms and indicating the wrong relationship types.

37. <u>D</u> is the correct answer.

The definition of a "city block," as given in the underlined portion, is only LOOSELY related to the content and does not help the writer to explain how the parade began and how it was organized. Choose D and eliminate C by this logic. The writer does not mention a "city block" in any detail elsewhere (eliminating A) and does not clearly explain how the size of a city block would be linked to the challenges faced by the parade organizers (eliminating B).

38. <u>C</u> is the correct answer.

The prompt requires an example of different New York businesses or institutions working together: a loan of animals from the Central Park Zoo to the Macy's Parade would be an example of collaboration. Choose C and eliminate A (visitors), B (Macy's employees, not employees from elsewhere in the city), and D (the pride of city officials, NOT the collaborative measures that they took) as answers that raise somewhat related issues that do NOT fit the specific prompt.

39. C is the correct answer.

Watch for redundancy in this question. A features redundancy with "massive," B needlessly defines the common term "inflated," and D features awkward, repetitive content with "situated" and "there." Only C avoids repetition while presenting (unlike B) the precise, new information about Central Park.

40. D is the correct answer.

The underlined verb should take the subject "Charlie Brown and the Grinch" in an inverted subject-verb combination. D is appropriately plural, while A, B, and C are all singular and should be eliminated.

41. C is the correct answer.

While sentence 8 describes "balloon handlers" in some detail, sentence 3 introduces the topic of the people who "guide" each balloon. Choose C to group the topics and eliminate A, B, and D, all of which would disrupt discussions of the balloons THEMSELVES and divide up linked information about the balloon handlers.

42. B is the correct answer.

So far in the passage, the writer has mentioned that the parade spectacles can represent classic cartoon characters (eliminating A and D, previous paragraph) and "current Broadway musicals" (eliminating C, paragraph that contains the underlined portion). Corporate sponsorship BEYOND Macy's itself has not been directly discussed at any point, so that B is an appropriate answer.

43. D is the correct answer.

In context, the "floats" are "Designed to be elaborate and colorful." Choose D to properly coordinate the descriptions and to avoid a misplaced modifier. A, B, and C all wrongly describe places where the floats are constructed, NOT the floats themselves, as "Designed" to have specific enjoyable properties.

44. D is the correct answer.

The proper parallelism for the underlined portion is "continues" and "concludes," so that both verbs effectively refer back to "It" (the Macy's Parade). Choose D and eliminate A, B, and C as breaking this required parallelism and as using constructions that (despite repeating the preposition "to") do not clearly pair off two present-tense verbs as a main structure.

NOTE: Passage 2, "A Home Turf for TIRF Microscopy," is adapted from "Better together: Merged microscope offers unprecedented look at biological processes in living cells." 7 May 2018, National Institute of Biomedical Imaging and Bioengineering. https://www.nibib.nih.gov/news-events/newsroom/better-together-merged-microscope-offers-unprecedented-look-biological-0. Accessed 19 June 2018.

Test 5

Writing and Language

2018 SAT Practice

Test 5

Writing and Language Test

35 MINUTES, 44 QUESTIONS

Turn to Section 2 of your answer sheet to answer the questions in this section.

Questions 1-11 are based on the following passage.

Trick or . . . Intellectual Property?

Americans will spend an estimated 9.1 billion dollars on Halloween this year, and yet many trick-or-treaters don't even have the tiniest inkling that this holiday is crawling with countless instances of

See Page 134 for the citation for this text.

1

A) NO CHANGE
B) are in the dark about the idea
C) can't even see, sense, or feel
D) remain unaware

intellectual property (IP). Examples range from the registered trademarks protecting the candy you eat and the costumes you wear, to the utility and design patents behind the tools to carve pumpkins or manufacture Halloween decorations. Every October, the U.S. Patent and Trademark Office (USPTO) uses social media as [2] a fun and accessible, and it is also a timely way to educate the public about the importance of IP and how it impacts their everyday lives.

[3] [1] Seven years ago, the USPTO decided to explore the deepest and darkest corners of more than two centuries worth of the patent and trademark archive. [2] Employees unearthed some particularly Halloween-appropriate patents and trademarks. [3] These workers' efforts were the starting points of a campaign that became known as "Creepy IP." [4] With items that include the trademark for Ghostbusters® Count Chocula® cereal, a sound mark for Darth Vader®, and patents for the electric extraction of poison or a flesh brushing apparatus from the 1880s, the USPTO's public records are full of interesting inventions and commercialized products. [5] Varied though they are, many of these items would fit right in at your local haunted house. [4]

2

A) NO CHANGE
B) a fun and also accessible, as well as timely
C) a fun way, and an accessible and timely
D) a fun, accessible, and timely

3

At this point in the passage, the writer is considering inserting the following sentence.

> Though perhaps the most popular program of its kind, the Patent and Trademark Office's Halloween offering does have important precedents.

Should the writer insert this content here?

A) Yes, because it helps the writer to explain how the "Creepy IP" initiative operates.
B) Yes, because it resolves a point of uncertainty that arose in the previous paragraph.
C) No, because it applies a wrongly critical tone to a program that the writer praises elsewhere.
D) No, because it raises an issue that the write does not pursue as the passage continues.

4

To make the order of ideas in the paragraph most logical, sentence 5 should be placed

A) where it is now.
B) after sentence 1.
C) after sentence 2.
D) after sentence 3.

CONTINUE

Test 5

Since its initial launch in October 2011, the #CreepyIP hashtag remains one of the USPTO's most successful interactive social media campaigns. Other federal agencies, private companies, the press, and members of the general public [5] have developed similar hastags in order to "personalize" the hunt for Halloween IP. This year, the USPTO [6] has even got other international IP offices to search their archives for Creepy IP.

Part of the USPTO's [7] mission is to educate: the public about the importance of IP, and Creepy IP generates tremendous awareness by highlighting how patents and trademarks are ingrained in our daily lives.

5

Which choice best supports the writer's depiction of the Creepy IP initiative at this point in the passage?

A) NO CHANGE

B) routinely use the hashtag to share the IP that they find spooky or intriguing.

C) network regularly with patent offices in other countries to locate forms of IP related to other holidays.

D) no longer see social media as mind-numbing or uninformative thanks to Creepy IP.

6

A) NO CHANGE

B) have even got

C) has even gotten

D) have even gotten

7

A) NO CHANGE

B) mission is to educate, the public

C) mission is, to educate the public

D) mission is to educate the public

CONTINUE

Innovation and creative endeavors are indispensable elements that drive economic growth and sustain the [8] competitive (and sometimes creepy) edge of the U.S. economy. [9] Instead, nationally-enforced IP protection provides incentives to invent and protects innovators from unauthorized use of their creepy inventions. The importance of IP to our economy is illustrated [10] from a major study by the Economics and Statistics Administration which found that, in 2014, IP-intensive industries directly and indirectly supported over 45 million jobs (nearly a third of all U.S. jobs) and over 38% of our national GDP. [11]

8

A) NO CHANGE
B) competitive (and sometimes creepy edge) of
C) competitive (and sometimes creepy edge of)
D) competitive (and sometimes creepy edge of

9

A) NO CHANGE
B) Nonetheless,
C) In turn,
D) Still,

10

A) NO CHANGE
B) for
C) by
D) to

11

Which choice offers the best concluding statement for the passage as a whole?

A) These figures were corroborated by a study that the USPTO conducted a few years later, as well as by a 2017 report from the Congressional Budget Office.

B) IP development is an important business, even if (as Creepy IP demonstrates) IP itself is at the core of lighthearted holiday fun.

C) Such figures can put to rest the qualms of those who regard Creepy IP and similar efforts as mere diversions.

D) Moreover, IP-intensive industries may become more profitable in the next five to ten years.

CONTINUE

Test 5

Questions 12-22 are based on the following passage.

Mastering the World of Chess

You don't need to be an expert to immerse yourself in the world of chess. School chess clubs, community chess programs, online play, and chess clubs like the Marshall Club in New York City all work to increase the [12] amount of people involved in the game and improve the level of play. However, [13] a person who becomes a high-earning professional in the field of chess competition is a great challenge.

The FIDE or the World Chess Federation is an international organization that works as a governing body for international chess competition and also connects national chess federations all around the globe. [14] For U.S.-based chess players, though, the role of FIDE is relatively minor. The United States Chess Federation (USCF) is the body that [15] looks at chess competitions in the United States and also represents the U.S. in FIDE. In 2016, the USCF had a membership of over 85,000 individuals.

12

A) NO CHANGE
B) amount for
C) number of
D) number for

13

A) NO CHANGE
B) people who become
C) if you become
D) becoming

14

The writer wishes to add details that support the paragraph's analysis of FIDE. Which choice accomplishes this goal?

A) NO CHANGE
B) Since 2012, the basic structure of FIDE has changed considerably.
C) In 2017, 185 nations and states maintained membership in FIDE.
D) The founding ideals of FIDE have also inspired nation-specific chess organizations.

15

Which choice most appropriately indicates that the USCF has been granted important responsibilities?

A) NO CHANGE
B) governs
C) is there for
D) approaches

CONTINUE

16 The designation of "Master in Chess" is a title that is awarded by the FIDE or by a national chess organization. "Master in Chess" is an official title for someone who is accepted as an expert player. "Grandmaster" is a chess title for even better players. In November of 2017, the FIDE released a rating list that included 1594 Grandmasters, with 1559 males and 35 females. Of these approximately 1,600 Grandmasters playing at present, there **17** is relative few people who play professionally, only about 10%. Each of these professional and elite players has earned a rating of over 2,700.

16

Which choice best combines the underlined sentences?

A) There is an official title for someone who is accepted as an expert player, and this title is the designation of "Master in Chess" as awarded by the FIDE or by a national chess organization.

B) The designation of "Master in Chess," an official title for someone who is accepted as an expert player, is awarded by the FIDE or by a national chess organization.

C) There is the designation of "Master in Chess," awarded by the FIDE or by a national chess organization, and it is a title as well for someone who is accepted as an expert chess player.

D) The designation of "Master in Chess" is awarded by the FIDE or by a national chess organization; it is a title, and it is also awarded for someone who is accepted as an expert chess player.

17

A) NO CHANGE

B) are relative

C) is relatively

D) are relatively

CONTINUE

There has been an uptick in the number of active players who have earned FIDE ratings. In 2009, there were 64,630; in 2011 the number of individuals increased to 86,029, and in 2013 there were 101,367. [18] Becoming a professional chess player takes distinctive talent and long-term training. For instance, Bobby Fischer (1943-2008), who hailed from Brooklyn, New York, showed an early ability for [19] chess yet learned the rules of the game at age 6. His first recorded tournament was played at the age of 12 and he attained the title of International Grandmaster at the age of 15. He [20] could become the United States Champion eight times in the course of eight attempts from 1957 to 1966.

18

Which choice provides the most effective introduction to the paragraph?

A) NO CHANGE

B) Famous chess players are often as well-known for their "outlandish" personal lives as for their actual skill.

C) Training in competitive chess typically starts much earlier than does training in other competitive games.

D) Often, chess Masters and Grandmasters pursue chess for reasons other than worldwide fame.

19

A) NO CHANGE

B) chess so long as he

C) chess and

D) chess or

20

A) NO CHANGE

B) became

C) has become

D) will have become

CONTINUE

The Chess World Cup is considered one of the most prestigious competitions for top players. In 2017, it was a 128-player, single-elimination contest that was won by a grandmaster from Armenia, Levon Aronian. He had won the tournament once before, in 2005. The total amount of prize money awarded to competitors is typically $1,600,000—with the runner-up taking home $80,000 and the winner earning $120,000. According to the tournament regulations, each player was responsible for [21] their own personal travel expenses and 20% of their winnings must be given back to FIDE. [22]

21

A) NO CHANGE
B) its
C) one's
D) his or her

22

The writer wishes to conclude the passage by connecting the content in this paragraph to the topic of non-expert chess players. Which choice most effectively accomplishes this goal?

A) Despite the high stakes and the sheer passion that chess tournaments inspire among the most seasoned chess players, such events remain relatively unknown outside a small community of high-ranking enthusiasts.

B) Such high-stakes prize money is a secondary benefit for many true "Masters in Chess," who see chess as a supreme intellectual challenge that transcends national and linguistic boundaries.

C) Although only a handful of chess players will ever rise to the top of such tournaments, these events draw together the worldwide community of chess enthusiasts, from "Masters in Chess" to eager novices.

D) Even as other fields of activity (such as competitive video gaming) adopt similar formats, chess remains exemplary as a deceptively simple, infinitely complex game of skill.

CONTINUE

Test 5

Questions 23-33 are based on the following passage and supplementary material.

A Devilish Question of Survival

Tasmanian devils are carnivorous marsupials, a type of mammal unique to Australia and Tasmania. Since European colonization, devils have become extinct on Australia and survive only on the island of Tasmania. However, they have fared better than another indigenous carnivore, the **23** wolf-like thylacine.

23

The writer is considering revising and expanding the underlined portion to read as follows.

> wolf-like thylacine, better known as the Tasmanian tiger, which was hunted to total extinction in the early 20th century.

Should the writer make use of the revised version?

A) Yes, because it helps to clarify the writer's argument and explains in detail a topic that is given additional attention in the next paragraph.

B) Yes, because it both adds relevant detail and helps to differentiate the situation of the wolf-like thylacine from that of the Tasmanian devil.

C) No, because it directly contradicts the writer's portrayal of the Tasmanian devil's situation as unique.

D) No, because it is excessively wordy and adds needlessly technical vocabulary to a passage that is meant to be approachable.

CONTINUE

Despite surviving the early influx of European settlers, [24] devils have encountered a new threat in recent years. In 1996, scientists identified a rare, contagious cancer, known as devil facial tumor disease (DTFD), that has since diminished devils' wild numbers from 150,000 [25] against only 30,000, a dramatic loss. Devils have especially low genetic diversity, which means that many animals have similar immune systems and therefore similar disease susceptibilities, so they are highly vulnerable to the cancer.

24

A) NO CHANGE

B) recent years have made devils encounter a new threat.

C) a new threat has encountered devils in recent years.

D) devils' new threat has been encountered in recent years.

25

A) NO CHANGE

B) for

C) at

D) to

CONTINUE

Test 5

[1] For years, scientists have been quarantining healthy devils in the hopes of reintroducing these animals into the wild as evidence of the disease disappears. [2] This method has several significant drawbacks, however. [3] For one thing, biologists cannot know for sure that the disease and all **26** its' carriers have disappeared at any given point. [4] Also, the numbers of devils bred in captivity could simply be too **27** microscopic for the wild population to ever surge back from near-extinction. [5] Upon reintroduction, the captive-bred devils may have trouble becoming established in environments where other animals are living in their habitats and consuming their food sources. **28**

26

A) NO CHANGE
B) it's
C) its
D) its's

27

A) NO CHANGE
B) unimpressive
C) detrimental
D) small

28

The writer would like to insert the following sentence in order to improve the paragraph.

> Furthermore, other species could fill the devils' ecological role if wild devil populations were to disappear.

For the most effective order of ideas, this sentence should be inserted

A) before sentence 1.
B) after sentence 3.
C) before sentence 5.
D) after sentence 5.

CONTINUE

New research, however, suggests that Tasmanian devils might be [29] making a go of the situation on their own. One team of researchers analyzed the genetics of wild devils. These researchers discovered that genes that promote strong immune [30] systems which can curb cancer growth, seem to have gained prominence in a variety of wild populations since the disease's arrival. This finding implies that the disease's high virulence [31] exert evolutionary pressure, so that devils with greater resistance to the cancer face more favorable prospects.

29

A) NO CHANGE
B) getting it right
C) recovering effectively
D) ameliorating shrewdly

30

A) NO CHANGE
B) systems those
C) systems, which
D) systems, those

31

A) NO CHANGE
B) to exert
C) exerting
D) has exerted

CONTINUE

Another group of researchers, this time from the University of Tasmania, has [32] successfully vaccinated 95 percent of a sample of 62 devils, all of which were released into the wild after testing positive for DTFD antibodies, which allow the devils' immune systems to attack cancer cells before these cells proliferate. Until the publication of these findings, some observers were beginning to doubt that a vaccine was even possible, but [33] with its approximate 95 percent success rate across multiple devil populations the University of Tasmania team is optimistic, and is now refining the vaccine to bring the required number of vaccines down from two to just one.

32

Which choice offers an accurate interpretation of the findings recorded in the graph?

A) NO CHANGE

B) successfully vaccinated 95 percent of a sample of 52 devils,

C) successfully vaccinated 85 percent of a sample of 62 devils,

D) successfully vaccinated 85 percent of a sample of 52 devils,

33

According to the graph, which choice best reflects the conditions of the research project?

A) NO CHANGE

B) with its approximate 90 percent success rate across multiple devil populations

C) with a success rate that fluctuates between 92 and 97 percent within one devil population sample

D) with a success rate that fluctuates between 80 and 97 percent within one devil population sample

Comparison of Two Tasmanian Devil Vaccination Projects

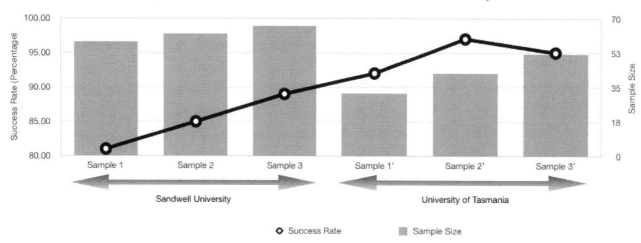

Questions 34-44 are based on the following passage.

Nam June Paik: Becoming a Legend

One of the most endearing touches in the recent exhibition *Nam June Paik: Becoming Robot* is a wall-sized photograph which shows Paik—video artist, performance artist, and [34] all-around—master of the ridiculous, sprawled among snaking electric cords and defunct television sets. He confidently looks up at the ceiling, a grin on his face that seems at once blissful and knowing, [35] his hands raised in something like victory.

34

A) NO CHANGE

B) all-around master—of the ridiculous, sprawled among

C) all-around master of the ridiculous—sprawled among

D) all-around master of the ridiculous, sprawled among

35

Which choice presents a second detail from the photograph of Paik that is most similar to the details already introduced in the sentence?

A) NO CHANGE

B) his surroundings heavily shadowed and sometimes obscured.

C) his devices clustered around him like adoring servants.

D) his reputation as a merry-making rebel by now indisputable.

CONTINUE

Test 5

The same attitude of exaltation and silliness is struck repeatedly throughout the *Becoming Robot* retrospective, which the Asia Society Museum staged in 2014. As a whole, the showcase casts Paik as a canny entertainer, a weirdly prophetic commentator, and a man with a **36** fascinating personality, being generally. Alas, it is impossible to meet Paik in person; he died in 2006, leaving behind a miniature universe **37** of recorded spectacles, wearable televisions, and golem-like robots. In *Becoming Robot*, the Paik personality lives on.

Born in South Korea and educated in Japan and Germany, Paik eventually found a home with other artists who combined medium-bending inquiry **38** with good-natured nonsense. Among his comrades in art were composer John Cage and dance impresario Merce Cunningham, **39** both known for the minimalistic and seemingly absurd compositions that they created. He also finds a kindred spirit in Asia Society curator Michelle Yun, whose approach in *Becoming Robot* is crisp, lyrical, and never too solemn.

36

A) NO CHANGE
B) fascinatingly, generally personality.
C) personality, generally and fascinating.
D) generally fascinating personality.

37

The writer is considering deleting the underlined portion and ending the sentence with a period after "universe." Should the underlined content be kept or deleted?

A) Kept, because it features relevant descriptions of specific Paik accomplishments.
B) Kept, because it addresses a counter-argument.
C) Deleted, because its tone is distractingly informal.
D) Deleted, because it reiterates previous information from an earlier paragraph.

38

A) NO CHANGE
B) for
C) to
D) as

39

A) NO CHANGE
B) both of whom were Paik colleagues known for their minimalistic, possibly irrational, seemingly absurd compositions.
C) both known for their minimalistic and seemingly absurd compositions.
D) both known as Paik colleagues.

CONTINUE

[1] Paik had an entire clique of robots at his disposal. He created Robot K-456 (1964), a jumble of lattices and circuits that was programmed to walk and talk, then crafted *Family of Robot* (1986). [2] A father, mother, and baby make up this ensemble, each family member **40** is composed of stacked televisions. [3] These creations, indeed, are ominous and otherworldly. [4] Elsewhere in his work, Paik was determined to seem more upbeat. [5] His chummy embrace of a technological present reached its peak in the televised special *Good Morning Mr. Orwell*, a vaudevillian rebuttal of George Orwell's dire futuristic novel *1984*. **41**

40

A) NO CHANGE

B) are composed

C) would be composed

D) composed

41

The writer wishes to add the following sentence to the paragraph.

> Despite the friendly, "familial" title, Paik's robots are uniquely disconcerting in appearance.

For the most effective order of ideas, the best placement for this new content would be before

A) sentence 2.

B) sentence 3.

C) sentence 4.

D) sentence 5.

CONTINUE

Test 5

Paik's vision of the future was [42] off the charts: he envisioned a "video telephone" (similar to Skype), imagined a digital "graduation book" (similar to Facebook), and coined the term "electronic superhighway" well before the Internet existed. Nonetheless, [43] there was something abidingly self-doubting in an artist so reputedly carefree. A sense of the past unfolds tenderly in Paik's 1993 *Room for Charlotte Moorman*, an homage to one of Paik's art world friends. With its empty clothes and mementos of the just-deceased [44] Moorman performances', it is a reminder that much is lost even as technology gains. Even if technology does, as Paik's works indicate, often improve the world, we will not all live to see the splendid future that such technology promises.

42

A) NO CHANGE
B) beyond all speculation
C) remarkably prescient
D) super-smart

43

Which choice offers the best transition to the discussion that follows?

A) NO CHANGE
B) there was something ironically cynical in an artist so fascinated by human follies.
C) there was something fundamentally vulnerable in an artist so caught up in a world of unrealistic musings.
D) there was something backward-looking in an artist so enthusiastically forward-driven.

44

A) NO CHANGE
B) Moorman's performances
C) Moorman's performances'
D) Moorman's performance's

STOP
If you finish before time is called, you may check your work on this section only.
Do not turn to any other section.

Answer Key on the Next Page

Answer Key: Test 5

Passage 1		Passage 2		Passage 3		Passage 4	
1.	D	12.	C	23.	B	34.	C
2.	D	13.	D	24.	A	35.	A
3.	D	14.	C	25.	D	36.	D
4.	A	15.	B	26.	C	37.	A
5.	B	16.	B	27.	D	38.	A
6.	C	17.	D	28.	C	39.	C
7.	D	18.	A	29.	C	40.	D
8.	A	19.	C	30.	C	41.	B
9.	C	20.	B	31.	D	42.	C
10.	C	21.	D	32.	B	43.	D
11.	B	22.	C	33.	A	44.	B

Topic Areas by Question

Expression of Ideas

Passage 1: Questions 1, 3-5, 9, 11

Passage 2: Questions 14-16, 18-19, 22

Passage 3, Questions 23, 27-29, 32-33

Passage 4, Questions 35, 37, 39, 41-43

Standard English Conventions

Passage 1: Questions 2, 6-8, 10

Passage 2: Questions 12-13, 17, 20-21

Passage 3, Questions 24-26, 30-31

Passage 4, Questions 34, 36, 38, 40, 44

Answer Explanations
Test 5, Pages 108-124

Passage 1, Pages 108-111

1. D is the correct answer.

For questions about writing style, try for concise wording that fits the tone of the passage. D precisely conveys the idea that Americans "remain unaware" of Halloween-related IP. A, B, and C all use wordier and inappropriately informal expressions for the same idea.

2. D is the correct answer.

When listed in series, three items should take similar grammar in order to obey standard parallelism: the proper format is "ITEM 1, ITEM 2, and ITEM 3." D is the only answer that adheres to these conventions, while A, B, and C insert additional linkages (instances of "and") that result in awkward constructions.

3. D is the correct answer.

The paragraph explains how the USPTO program works, but does NOT call attention to any of the program's "precedents" as mentioned in the proposed sentence. Choose D for this reason, and eliminate A and B because the idea of "precedents" is a new topic or a loose end (rather than a way of strengthening the writer's explanations. C is inaccurate because noting that a program has "precedents" is not the same as criticizing it for being unoriginal; eliminate this answer for applying a negative tone to a neutral statement.

4. A is the correct answer.

Sentence 5 refers back to specific items that are "Varied" and that would fit in at a haunted house; sentence 4 lists such items, so that A is the best answer. Neither sentence 1 nor sentence 3 explicitly mentions any items (eliminating B and D), while sentence 2 only refers to "patents and trademarks" and provides no basis for noting that the items are "Varied" (eliminating trap answer C).

5. <u>B</u> is the correct answer.

The Creepy IP campaign involves an "interactive" search for interesting items related to Halloween; B thus continues the discussion of this campaign's hashtag in a manner that reflects the nature of the campaign. Choose this answer and eliminate A ("other hashtags," a topic that is not raised or pursued elsewhere), C ("other holidays," another distraction from the writer's discussion), and D (argumentative rather than informative in content).

6. <u>C</u> is the correct answer.

The USPTO is a single organization and should thus take the singular verb "has"; moreover, when used with "has" as an auxiliary verb, "to get" should take the form "gotten." C is the only appropriate answer. A and B both use the improper form "got," while B and D are both plural.

7. <u>D</u> is the correct answer.

The underlined portion should be one unified idea that indicates what, exactly, the mission of the USPTO is. D properly and fluidly explains that the USPTO's mission is to educate the public. A breaks up these ideas with an improper colon usage, while B and C break up the same ideas with unnecessary and improper commas.

8. <u>A</u> is the correct answer.

Any parenthetical phrase should feature both an opening parenthesis and a closing parenthesis, and should allow for a grammatically correct sentence in the event that it is deleted. A fulfills both requirements, since the deletion of the parenthetical phrase properly results in "competitive . . . edge." B wrongly results in "competitive . . . of" if the parenthetical phrase is deleted, C wrongly results in "competitive . . . the," and D only features one parenthesis.

9. <u>C</u> is the correct answer.

The underlined portion serves as a transition for two sentences that describe complementary benefits in terms of the national economy and the innovations of inventors. C properly calls attention to benefits that work together or "In turn." A, B, and D all indicate contrasts or exceptions and are thus incorrect.

10. <u>C</u> is the correct answer.

The proper idiomatic phrase for describing a source that illustrates a point is "illustrated by." Choose C and eliminate A and D (both of which would indicate direction or movement). B wrongly indicates that the "major study" is the one RECEIVING the illustration, not that it PROVIDES an illustration for readers.

11. <u>B</u> is the correct answer.

While the paragraph that contains the underlined portion relates IP to important economic factors, earlier paragraphs focus on the entertaining aspects of the Creepy IP initiative. B properly draws these topics together and reflects the discussion in the passage "as a whole." A and D provide new information about the economic situation rather than RETURNING to earlier points, while C raises possible criticisms of Creepy IP that the writer avoids.

Passage 2, Pages 112-115

12. <u>C</u> is the correct answer.

Because "people" can be counted, they are described using the word "number," not "amount." Eliminate A and B and choose C, which properly describes the number "of" people involved. D, "for," is idiomatically incorrect and would wrongly indicate that the "number" is given to the people as a possession or a goal.

13. <u>D</u> is the correct answer.

The underlined portion should, for the sake of logical reference, describe something that "is a challenge," such as "becoming" a high-earning professional. D is correct, while A and B wrongly equate individuals with an abstract thing or "challenge. C wrongly places a phrase starting with "if" in parallel with the noun "challenge."

14. <u>C</u> is the correct answer.

The writer explains that FIDE has a presence "all around the globe," so that calling attention to the number of "nations" involved would offer an appropriate further detail. Choose C and eliminate A (which wrongly downplays the FIDE's importance), B (which focuses on its structure, not its influence), and D (which mentions the FIDE's principles, a topic that is not mentioned in the existing content).

15. <u>B</u> is the correct answer.

If the USCF has important supervisory responsibilities, it would naturally "govern" chess competitions. Choose B as a word that calls attention to the topic or theme of authority, which A (observation), C (presence), and D (movement) do NOT raise in any direct fashion.

16. <u>B</u> is the correct answer.

The two sentences should be combined to explain the topic of a "Master in Chess" title in a concise and well-coordinated manner. B is an effective answer, since it consolidates information (does not mention the title twice, for instance) and features a well-structured interrupting phrase that explains that "Master in Chess" is "an official title." A references the "title" repeatedly and awkwardly, while C and D incorporate awkward instances of phrases such as "There is" and "it is" rather than presenting the fundamental information about the "Master in Chess" title efficiently.

17. D is the correct answer.

The verb in the underlined portion should describe the "people" and should thus be plural, while the second word should describe HOW few people there are and should thus be an adverb. Choose D, and eliminate A and C for using singular verbs. A and B wrongly use the adjective "relative," not the adverb "relatively."

18. A is the correct answer.

The information after the underlined portion describes Bobby Fischer, who showed "early ability" and increased his prowess in chess over several years. Thus, A is an effective fit for this discussion of the "talent" and "training" of a specific player. Fischer's personality (eliminating B) and motives (eliminating D) are not mentioned, nor are any games other than chess (eliminating C).

19. C is the correct answer.

The sentence presents two related facts about Fischer's early-age chess activities, so that C properly uses "and" to connect these similar pieces of information. A wrongly indicates a contrast, B indicates a condition rather than an accomplished fact, and D wrongly sets up alternatives.

20. B is the correct answer.

The paragraph as a whole presents Fischer's chess accomplishments in past tense, so that B properly continues the agreement of tenses. A describes a possible condition, NOT an accomplished historical fact. C indicates past action that continues to the present, NOT a concluded past accomplishment, while D indicates something that is designated to happen at a point in the future.

21. D is the correct answer.

The underlined portion should refer back to "each player," a singular noun that takes the possessive "his or her." Choose D and eliminate A (plural) and B (used for non-human things). C is a singular third-person possessive, but can only refer back to earlier instances of the pronoun "one," NOT to a person named by a noun for a single person.

22. C is the correct answer.

The prompt requires a reference to "non-expert chess players," which C fulfills with its reference to "eager novices." Choose this answer and eliminate A and B, which only refer to expert chess players. D does refer to chess ITSELF as a game that can seem "deceptively simple," but this reference should not be mistaken for a reference to the non-expert PLAYERS who are part of the chess community.

Passage 3, Pages 116-120

23. <u>B</u> is the correct answer.

The proposed expansion of the underlined content further describes the "wolf-like thylacine" by linking it to Tasmania and explaining that, unlike the still-extant Tasmanian devil, this animal is now extinct. B reflects the relevant nature of this material, while A wrongly indicates that the wolf-like thylacine (which is mentioned nowhere else in the passage) is discussed in the NEXT paragraph. C wrongly indicates that the Tasmanian devil is compared to a large number of animals (and is thus "unique") instead of to just the wolf-like thylacine, while D mis-characterizes this clear and understandable presentation of scientific information.

24. <u>A</u> is the correct answer.

The underlined portion should align with the modifier, which describes an animal as "surviving." The [Tasmanian] devils would naturally survive, so choose A and eliminate B (indicating that "years" survived) as well as C and D (indicating that a "threat" survived). The false answers all create misplaced modifiers.

25. <u>D</u> is the correct answer.

The proper expression for comparing a change in number is "from [first number] to [second number]," a phrasing that is properly reflected in D. Choose this answer, and eliminate all the others as idiomatically incorrect or as indicating false relationships such as antagonism (A), possession or purpose (B), and place (C).

26. <u>C</u> is the correct answer.

For the underlined portion, a possessive indicating a "disease" (which takes the pronoun "it") that has carriers is required. C, "its," is the proper possessive, while B is the contraction of "it is" and A and C are nonexistent forms.

27. <u>D</u> is the correct answer.

In context, the underlined adjective should refer back to the "numbers" of Tasmanian devils bred in captivity. If these numbers are not large enough to enable a "surge," they would naturally be "small." Choose D as the most natural fit. A (ability to be detected), B (reputation) and trap answer C (damage or harm, NOT size) all involve inappropriate contexts, and in some cases apply too harshly negative tones to the "numbers."

28. <u>C</u> is the correct answer.

The proposed sentence refers to the overall "ecological role" of the devils, which other species could fill, while sentence 5 more specifically explains that "other animals" would take over the devils' habitats and food sources. Choose C, and eliminate A and B as answers that would disrupt the discussion of devils in captivity (NOT in their role in the wild). D would wrongly place sentence 5 AFTER specifics that it should introduce.

29. C is the correct answer.

The underlined portion describes Tasmanian devils, which (in context) are clearly showing resistance to a disease that has afflicted them. These animals would thus be "recovering," so that C is an appropriate answer. A and B are overly informal in style, while D ("shrewdly," meaning "cleverly") raises an inappropriate context.

30. C is the correct answer.

The sentence that contains the underlined portion features the subject-verb phrase "genes . . . seem," which by standard convention should NOT be split by only a single unit of punctuation. C properly offsets the phrase "which can curb cancer growth" using two commas, while A and B create incorrect single-comma versions of the sentence. B and D wrongly insert a full independent clause, "those can curb cancer growth," into a full sentence without a proper transition.

31. D is the correct answer.

The verb "exert" refers to a "disease," which appeared in the past ("since the disease's arrival") and has been present in Tasmanian devil populations up to recent times. Choose D (the proper form for past-into-present action) and eliminate A as indicating present action only. B and C both wrongly create sentence fragments.

32. B is the correct answer.

The underlined portion should reflect the findings of the research team from "the University of Tasmania," which in Sample 3' successfully vaccinated 95% of a sample of slightly fewer than 53 Tasmanian devils. B reflects this information. A and C indicate higher sample sizes than the University of Tasmania team used, while C and D reflect lower success rates: in general, these answers confuse the University of Tasmania figures with the Sandwell University figures.

33. A is the correct answer.

The underlined portion should refer to the University of Tasmania team, with its approximate 92-93% (Sample 1'), 97-98% (Sample 2') and 95% (Sample 3') success rates. An average of 95% would be a fair estimate across these samples. Choose A and eliminate B as too low of an estimate. C and D refer to the wrong quantity: the success rate differs across THREE devil populations, not "within one" as these answers claim.

Passage 4, Pages 121-124

34. C is the correct answer.

The expression between the dashes should be coordinated so that its deletion would result in a grammatically coherent sentence, and should ideally obey three-item parallelism. C ("artist . . . artist . . . master") fulfills both conditions. Choose this answer and eliminate A (which breaks the parallelism by placing "master" outside the dashes) and B (which results in the improper wording "Paik . . . of the ridiculous" when the content between dashes is deleted). D wrongly uses a comma instead of a dash to close off the phrase, which itself contains commas and is best coordinated using dashes for clarity.

35. A is the correct answer.

The sentence refers to where Paik "looks" and to his "grin": a reference to another gesture, such as the gesture of his hands, would serve as a similar detail. Choose A, and eliminate B and C (both of which are closer to details from the PREVIOUS sentence). D refers to Paik's reputation, a topic of the passage as a whole but not of the specific sentence that requires additional details.

36. D is the correct answer.

The underlined portion should exhibit proper adjective and adverb references. In D, the adverb "generally" properly modifies the adjective "fascinating," which itself describes "personality." Choose this answer. Both A and B wrongly position the adverb "generally" to modify the NOUN "personality," while C wrongly attempts parallelism between an adverb ("generally") and an adjective ("fascinating").

37. A is the correct answer.

Because the underlined portion explains Paik's "universe" of accomplishments by providing specifics, this portion features relevant details. Choose A and eliminate B (since the underlined portion simply offers information and does NOT take a position). C wrongly characterizes this straightforward, explanatory content as "informal," while trap answer D misconstrues the content of the passage: Paik's involvement with technology was referenced earlier, but his "wearable" items and "robots" were NOT mentioned.

38. A is the correct answer.

The proper paired phrase for two things that are combined is "combined . . . with." Choose A, and eliminate B (purpose) and C (direction or ownership) both as breaking standard English usage and as indicating the wrong types of relationships. D also breaks standard usage and indicates comparison, not COMBINATION.

39. C is the correct answer.

This question requires the elimination of redundant content: "compositions" are naturally "created" (eliminating A) and something that is "possibly irrational" is naturally "seemingly absurd" (eliminating B). D, though short, creates redundancy between the terms "comrades in art" and "colleagues." Choose C as the best answer, and as one that offers useful information about Cage's and Cunningham's compositions.

40. <u>D</u> is the correct answer.

The underlined portion should refer back to "each family member" (singular) but should NOT initiate a new independent clause (and thus create a comma splice). D is thus the best answer since "composed" is treated as an adjective, not as part of a verb phrase as in A, B (which is also plural), or C.

41. <u>B</u> is the correct answer.

The proposed sentence should serve as a transition from a positive connotation ("familial," "friendly") to a negative one ("disconcerting"). While sentence 2 describes the ensemble *Family of Robot*, sentence 3 changes tone to describe the robots as "ominous" or troubling. Choose B and eliminate A (since sentence 2 does not feature a negative tone), C (which would place the proposed content after a statement that, with the word "indeed," is designed to RESPOND to it) and D (which would place the proposed content after, not within, the discussion of *Family of Robot*).

42. <u>C</u> is the correct answer.

In context, Paik is described as envisioning specific technologies before they existed: C, "prescient" or sensing the future, would properly characterize his vision. Choose this answer and eliminate A and D as too informal. B is illogical: something "beyond speculation" would be impossible to imagine, yet Paik's vision of the future was clear and specific.

43. <u>D</u> is the correct answer.

While the early stages of the paragraph describe Paik's vision of the future, the later portions examine his "sense of the past." D presents the proper contrast between "backward" and "forward." Choose this answer and eliminate A (self-doubting), B (cynical), and C (vulnerable), all of which CRITICIZE Paik rather than describing his specific responses to technology and to his friend Charlotte Moorman.

44. <u>B</u> is the correct answer.

The underlined portion should clarify what the "mementos" were "of" by providing a noun as the object of the preposition. Thus, the noun "performances" is appropriate, and the possessive "Moorman's" would properly indicate that Moorman gave the performances. Choose B and eliminate A (which indicates that the performances owned Moorman, not the other way around). C and D both feature only possessives, not the required noun.

NOTE: Passage 1, "Trick or . . . Intellectual Property," is adapted from "Something Spooky This Way Comes — Strange, Weird, and Unsettling IP." 30 October 2017, U.S. Patent and Trademark Office. https://www.commerce.gov/news/blog/2017/10/something-spooky-way-comes-strange-weird-and-unsettling-ip. Accessed 20 June 2018.

Test 6

Writing and Language
2018 SAT Practice

Test 6

Writing and Language Test

35 MINUTES, 44 QUESTIONS

Turn to Section 2 of your answer sheet to answer the questions in this section.

Questions 1-11 are based on the following passage.

Small Business, Good Technology, Big Problems?

Starting a small business in today's economy is perhaps easier then it was earlier in history, thanks in part to the resources that the Internet makes easily accessible to hard-working entrepreneurs or "start-up" business leaders. If you have a business concept, you can build a web site for that business on a user-friendly

1

A) NO CHANGE
B) easiest, than
C) easier than
D) more easy, then

CONTINUE

platform such as Wix or Wordpress. For help with marketing or logo design, you can hire a freelancer. Online advertising will also give your business visibility, and several options—such as Google AdWords— **2** they are optimal for early-stage businesses that don't have much cash on hand.

However, even if starting a small business is now extremely easy, building a small business into a profitable or well-known business remains a daunting task. **3** Apparently, the Internet is not as useful as is commonly believed. The same technologies that can facilitate the formation of a small business can lead to **4** a big kerfuffle that will consume time, money, and effort that could have been better invested elsewhere.

2
A) NO CHANGE
B) are optimal
C) which is optimal
D) is optimal

3
Which choice provides the most effective transition to the discussion that follows?
A) NO CHANGE
B) Arguably, the Internet is linked to the flaws of some companies.
C) Surprisingly, business owners are turning against Internet-based entrepreneurship.
D) Stunningly, Internet marketing mostly attracts negative publicity.

4
Which choice most appropriately preserves the style and tone of the passage?
A) NO CHANGE
B) nothing but one awful idea after another
C) a real tragedy on our hands
D) a series of poor decisions

CONTINUE

Because the Internet makes entrepreneurship so easy, [5] they will be formed based on questionable premises. An entrepreneur with little background in technology but with enough money to create a robust early-stage technology business—an amount, for instance, of $100,000 or more—can begin [6] finding facilities for an exceptionally large and luxurious office space. Such a technology company can quickly become [7] unmanageable, although the entrepreneur lacks the technology expertise to oversee the work of the various employees in a comprehending, efficient manner.

5

A) NO CHANGE
B) that
C) each one of them
D) some businesses

6

Which choice introduces the information that is most closely and effectively related to the writer's discussion in this paragraph?

A) NO CHANGE
B) reaching out to publications that routinely profile important business leaders.
C) hiring freelance programmers or device engineers to create products.
D) formulating a set of business principles that are forward-thinking and inspirational.

7

A) NO CHANGE
B) unmanageable, because
C) unmanageable, and
D) unmanageable, or

CONTINUE

In another problematic scenario, a technology entrepreneur may have the intensive practical knowledge needed to create a well-designed product, but will then find himself or herself unable to market that product in a way that produces steady revenues. The developers of new smartphone applications (or "apps") and new online publications often find themselves in vexing positions of this sort. Crafting an application that is user-friendly is easy for **8** a well-coordinated team. Such a team possesses the right balance of marketing creativity and programming aptitude. The real challenge is making such an app stand out in what, admittedly, is a crowded marketplace for apps. A further challenge involves turning that app into a source of income, whether through selling ad space or through **9** the app to be bought by a larger company.

Although the obstacles to small business success in an Internet-based marketplace are undeniable, the Internet itself provides a few possible safeguards. Business mentors can be found on social networks such as LinkedIn. Moreover, **10** entrepreneurs who "rush into" unwise technology investments can use technology itself to compensate for some of their mistakes. The Internet can't automatically save a bad **11** business; it can, nonetheless, alert entrepreneurs to possible mis-steps and keep new enterprises on the right track.

8

Which choice best combines the sentences at the underlined portion?

A) a team, well-coordinated, and it is one that possesses

B) a well-coordinated team, such a team as having

C) well-coordinating a team which is one having

D) a well-coordinated team—one with

9

A) NO CHANGE

B) the position of the app

C) positioning the app

D) to position the app

10

The writer wishes to introduce a second example that functions like the example in the previous sentence. Which choice would be most appropriate?

A) NO CHANGE

B) local conferences offer aspiring entrepreneurs forums for sharing new ideas.

C) innovations in online publishing have lowered the printing costs for books on business topics.

D) web-accessible publications feature articles that offer guidance for early-stage businesses.

11

A) NO CHANGE

B) business, it can, nonetheless alert

C) business it can; nonetheless alert

D) business, it can, nonetheless; alert

CONTINUE

Test 6

Questions 12-22 are based on the following passage.

The Seeing Eye: Animal Service at Its Finest

[1] In 1927, Dorothy Harrison Eustis authored an article titled "The Seeing Eye" for the *Saturday Evening Post*. [2] Eustis was an American dog trainer living in Switzerland. [3] She wrote an account about a school in Germany that was training dogs to work with World War I veterans who were blinded in battle. [4] The program was relatively unknown in the United States at the time. [5] Although she received many letters from blind people, Eustis was particularly intrigued by **12** correspondence written by a 19-year old college student and salesman, Morris Frank. [6] In 1928, Frank traveled to Eustis's dog-training school in Switzerland, Fortunate Fields. [7] According to his letters, Frank not only wanted a dog to guide him but also hoped to start a school to train dogs **13** from other blind people. [8] There he was paired with his first guide dog, a German Shepherd named Buddy, and gained a new sense of independence. [9] Finally acquainted with one another in-person, Frank and Eustis worked together to establish the first guide dog school in the United States; the new institution opened in 1929. **14**

12

A) NO CHANGE
B) correspondence wrote
C) correspondence, which written
D) correspondence, which wrote

13

A) NO CHANGE
B) for
C) of
D) to

14

To make the order of ideas in the paragraph most logical, sentence 7 should be placed

A) where it is now.
B) after sentence 5.
C) after sentence 8.
D) after sentence 9.

CONTINUE

Today, The Seeing Eye is a very successful organization. The foundation's employees and volunteers breed and raise puppies to become Seeing Eye Dogs, train the dogs to guide blind people, and teach blind people the proper use, handling, and care of the dogs. **15** The organization also conducts and supports research that influences canine health and development. Guide dogs are an invaluable resource for visually impaired people who wish to live active, fulfilling lives. As of February of 2018, The Seeing Eye in Morristown, New Jersey, had matched 17,000 visually impaired individuals with Seeing Eye dogs.

People young and old **16** assess Seeing Eye puppies into their homes and raise these animals for roughly one year, often with support and guidance from local 4-H clubs. Individuals who raise puppies **17** also receive each dog's veterinary care free of charge. Puppy raisers **18** go right over to 4-H puppy club meetings with their dogs in order to work on basic obedience training and to socialize with the young dogs at these events.

15

The writer is considering deleting the underlined content. Should this sentence be kept or deleted?

A) Kept, because it appropriately defines one expected duty of a Seeing Eye volunteer.

B) Kept, because it appropriately continues the writer's discussion of The Seeing Eye's endeavors.

C) Deleted, because it distracts from the writer's discussion of Eustis and Frank.

D) Deleted, because it presents information that is repeated in the next paragraph.

16

A) NO CHANGE

B) accept

C) except

D) exempt

17

A) NO CHANGE

B) also receive complimentary veterinary care, free of charge for each dog.

C) also receive, for each dog that is being raised, complimentary veterinary care.

D) also receive each dog's veterinary care both in addition and free of charge.

18

A) NO CHANGE

B) sit there at

C) attend

D) get

CONTINUE

Test 6

The types of dogs that are bred and raised to be guide dogs **19** include, but are not limited, to German Shepherds Labrador Retrievers, and Golden Retrievers. Guide dogs are ultimately trained to be aware and to navigate various obstacles, but they are not able to interpret road signs or crossing signs. While the visually impaired owner is responsible for determining a destination and directing the dog, it is the dog's responsibility to get the owner there safely. The Americans for Disabilities Act, laws in all 50 states, and legislation in the provinces of Canada **20** provides that a Seeing Eye dog can accompany a blind person to all public places including restaurants, transportation centers, theaters, stores, and anywhere their masters need to go.

19

A) NO CHANGE

B) include, but are not limited to, German Shepherds,

C) include, but are not limited: to German Shepherds,

D) include but are not limited, to German Shepherds,

20

A) NO CHANGE

B) provide

C) that provide

D) which provide

CONTINUE

Some of the puppies that are raised for The Seeing Eye are not suitable to serve as guide dogs. [21] It is remarkable, when this fact is taken into account, that the Seeing Eye has done little to adjust its breeding practices since its founding. Once a dog displays full competency as a guide dog, each dog is matched with the right owner, who receives training to use it. The average working life for a Seeing Eye dog is seven to eight years.

One can only imagine the difference that Seeing Eye dogs have made in the lives of people like Morris Frank and so many thousands of others. [22] In response, the organization enables blind people all over the world to enjoy a sense of self-esteem and improved mobility.

21

Which choice most effectively builds upon the point that the writer introduced in the previous sentence?

A) NO CHANGE

B) Generally, successful Seeing Eye dogs exhibit superior powers of empathy and perception.

C) In the course of a lifetime, a single blind person may cycle through as many as twelve Seeing Eye dogs.

D) There may be behavioral or medical issues that prohibit a dog from being a responsible companion.

22

A) NO CHANGE

B) Nonetheless,

C) On the other hand,

D) Today,

CONTINUE

Test 6

Questions 23-33 are based on the following passage.

A Sensational Surprise from George Bernard Shaw

As a playwright, George Bernard Shaw is associated mostly with his dapper and fastidiously-observed social comedies. Present-day audiences know Shaw best from *Pygmalion*, or from one of the many adaptations of this work—a study of art and egotism titled after a Greek myth and centered on a [23] massively stuck-up language professor named Henry Higgins. Intellectualism, subtlety, and [24] occasional fussiness, define the trademark "Shaw-vian" style.

[25] According to literary scholars, Shaw would seem supremely unlikely to pen a sensational script: science fiction, a murder mystery, or a Revolutionary War melodrama. Astonishingly, Shaw did pen the last one of these. Written in 1896 and staged in New York the following year, Shaw's *The Devil's Disciple* is a tale of intrigue, mistaken identity, and morally fraught choices. Throughout, Shaw shines through as both a canny entertainer and an earnest moralist. [26] This drama demonstrates that Shaw's entire body of work has generally been underestimated and delivers rousing entertainment while doing so.

23
A) NO CHANGE
B) self-absorbed
C) full-of-himself
D) pesky

24
A) NO CHANGE
B) occasional fussiness define
C) occasional fussiness, defines
D) occasional fussiness defines

25
A) NO CHANGE
B) According to his own testimony,
C) Ironically,
D) Naturally,

26
The writer wishes to indicate that the negative traits specifically attributed to Shaw are open to dispute. Which choice best accomplishes this goal?

A) NO CHANGE
B) This drama hints that Shaw himself was uncomfortable with his reputation for "intellectualism"
C) This drama shows us that the fussy, finicky image of Shaw is deeply questionable
D) This drama proves that Shaw's work was never meant to have a single "core audience"

CONTINUE

In terms of staging, *The Devil's Disciple* is also unique. Shaw's other important works take place in drawing rooms; this play calls [27] <u>for settings, that include</u> gallows, town squares, and New England cottages. The ideal set for *The Devil's Disciple* is [28] <u>suited to</u> rushing, fighting, and stomping. Melodramas thrive on emphatic action, and this melodrama is no exception.

27

A) NO CHANGE
B) for settings that include
C) for settings, they include
D) for settings they include

28

A) NO CHANGE
B) most surely the place with
C) right in there for
D) worked up with

CONTINUE

[1] For all its liveliness, Shaw's play begins with dour circumstances. [2] The year is 1777, and the small town of Westerbridge, New Hampshire, is bracing itself for hostilities with the British army. [3] Into this commotion comes Richard Dudgeon, the Devil's Disciple of the title. [4] Richard is mostly interested in learning the contents of his father's will (which could make his fortune) and in shocking the good people of Westerbridge, including local minister Anthony Anderson and Anthony's poised young wife. [5] Each of these men **29** are convinced that the British army, intending to "make an example" of the rebels, will soon hang an inhabitant of Westerbridge. [6] The victim could be **30** a community leader like Anderson, or a miscreant like Dudgeon. [7] It is possible, too, that some other victim could be designated, goading these two prominent characters to heroic action. **31**

29

A) NO CHANGE
B) is
C) were
D) being

30

A) NO CHANGE
B) community leaders
C) that of a community leader
D) those of community leaders

31

The writer would like to add the following sentence to the paragraph.

> Despite their differences, Richard and Anthony do have one opinion in common.

For the most logical and effective order of ideas, this content should be placed after

A) sentence 4.
B) sentence 5.
C) sentence 6.
D) sentence 7.

CONTINUE

A melodrama of its time, *The Devil's Disciple* is full of suspenseful twists that 19th-century theatergoers might have seen coming, but that 21st-century viewers (with their very different narrative expectations) probably won't. **[32]** The second act is a masterwork of both unpredictability and cleverness; the tension rises, and so **[33]** does the amount of clever quips. As the end draws near, a few of Shaw's most set-in-their-ways characters manage to change radically. You might never think they had it in them—or that Shaw had a play like this in him, for that matter.

32

At this point in the passage, the writer is considering adding the following sentence.

> After all, most of Shaw's dramas are based on an appreciation of quiet ironies that today's fast-paced technology does not necessarily foster.

Should the writer insert this sentence?

A) Yes, because it offers a further description of an uncommon feature of *The Devil's Disciple*.

B) Yes, because it returns to the writer's argument that Shaw's talent has been wrongly underestimated.

C) No, because it moves away from analysis of *The Devil's Disciple* to consider Shaw's work at large.

D) No, because it offers unnecessary criticisms of Shaw's intended audience.

33

A) NO CHANGE

B) do the amount

C) does the number

D) do the number

CONTINUE

Test 6

Questions 34-44 are based on the following passage and supplementary material.

Undersea Mapping Finds Its Groove

Imagine dragging [34] one's outstretched fingers through wet beach sand, leaving long grooves behind. Scientists recently discovered enormous grooves buried under the sea floor near Costa Rica. The detailed three-dimensional data that researchers used to [35] detect these corrugations can help them better understand large subduction zone earthquakes and related tsunamis worldwide.

In an article published online by Nature Geoscience, researchers reported finding corrugations, or giant kilometers-long grooves, between the two tectonic plates that form part of the Costa Rica subduction zone. [36] Using a variety of technologies that were recently developed and that have proven useful in a range of important industries, scientists from the U.S. Geological Survey, University of California Santa Cruz, University of Texas, and McGill University produced an unprecedented, detailed view of the megathrust fault formed by these colliding and sliding plates.

See Page 160 for the citation for this text.

34

A) NO CHANGE

B) their

C) his or her

D) your

35

A) NO CHANGE

B) underscore

C) hunt down

D) ruminate on

36

The writer wishes to add new, relevant, and specific details that help to explain how the scientists conducted their research. Which choice accomplishes this goal?

A) NO CHANGE

B) Using an array of research tactics that, as explained in the Nature Geoscience article, were related to the detection of ocean grooves,

C) Using 3D seismic imaging techniques developed by the oil industry along with state-of-the-art computer visualization software,

D) Using research strategies that were informed by the collaborative nature of their multi-institutional effort,

CONTINUE

The study produced a detailed map showing Costa Rica and the [37] surrounding ocean, marked with a star, that pinpoints where scientists have been studying the ocean floor. This yellow star marks the spot where researchers reported finding corrugations, or giant grooves that are kilometers long, hundreds of meters wide, and tens of meters high. These corrugations are located between the Cocos [38] as well as Caribbean tectonic plates that form part of the Costa Rica subduction zone. [39]

37

A) NO CHANGE
B) surrounding ocean, marked with a star
C) surrounding ocean marked with a star,
D) surrounding ocean marked, with a star,

38

A) NO CHANGE
B) but also
C) and
D) to

39

At this point, the writer is considering inserting the following sentence.

> As the tourism industry has boomed in Central America and the Caribbean, reassuring travelers that they are staying at safe and well-monitored sites has become a priority.

Should the writer make this insertion here?

A) Yes, because it further explains a research motivation that the writer briefly suggested in the first paragraph.

B) Yes, because it introduces a specific event that helps the reader to form an emotional connection to the writer's topic.

C) No, because it loosely relates the core content of the passage to a topic that the writer does not pursue.

D) No, because it would best be placed later in the passage to support the writer's analysis of precautionary measures.

CONTINUE

Test 6

"Subduction zones are hugely important, both because of the hazards they pose and because they are [40] in which the earth destroys crust," said lead author Joel Edwards, a USGS student contractor pursuing a Ph.D. at UC Santa Cruz. "And megathrust faults, within subduction zones, host the largest earthquakes on the planet. They are more likely to generate tsunamis, which, as we saw from Japan and Sumatra, [41] can cause greater casualties in one blow than do *all* of the earthquakes in a single year." In the United States, subduction zones with megathrust faults exist offshore of Alaska, Washington, Oregon, Northern California, Puerto Rico, the US Virgin Islands, Guam, and the Northern Mariana Islands.

40

A) NO CHANGE
B) where
C) when
D) that

41

Which choice offers the most accurate interpretation of the data in the graph?

A) NO CHANGE
B) are more destructive than earthquakes but *rarely* inflict more than 50,000 casualties.
C) in almost *every* case inflict twice as many deaths as injuries when they strike.
D) almost always result in greater loss of life than does *any* given earthquake in *any* given year.

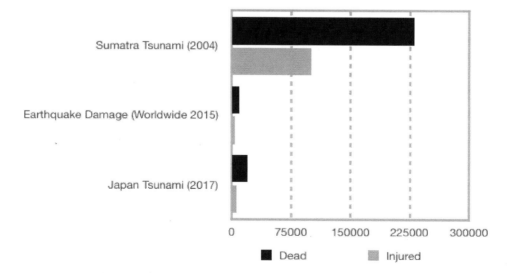

Fatalities from Natural Disasters

Sumatra Tsunami (2004)

Earthquake Damage (Worldwide 2015)

Japan Tsunami (2017)

0   75000   150000   225000   300000

■ Dead   ▨ Injured

CONTINUE

"Gently rolling hills and valleys that are parallel and stretch for miles," is how Edwards explained the scene would look if you [42] are able to stand on the fault surface looking across the grooves. In his words, "Corrugations are a great record of how blocks are sliding past each other along a fault." Scientists have found similar grooves at the base of fast moving glaciers and other faults, but not on megathrust faults.

[43] This type of imaging may have applications outside the realm of geology. Small changes in groove direction record a history of shifts in plate movement. [44] In contrast, the rougher areas indicate where the megathrust jumped to form a new fault, and hasn't had enough time to smooth the surface. Other details in the 3D seismic imaging data imply that the grooves trap fluids that could lubricate the fault and affect earthquake size and frequency.

42

Which choice introduces the proper wording to indicate that the writer is describing a purely hypothetical scenario?

A) NO CHANGE

B) were able

C) will be able

D) used to be able

43

Which choice best introduces the paragraph?

A) NO CHANGE

B) This unique, highly-detailed imaging revealed other buried secrets.

C) The present imaging innovations may, indeed, make further technological breakthroughs possible.

D) The imaging used by Edwards has set the groundwork for a second research effort.

44

A) NO CHANGE

B) Astonishingly,

C) In addition,

D) Of course,

STOP
If you finish before time is called, you may check your work on this section only.
Do not turn to any other section.

Answer Key: Test 6

Passage 1		Passage 2		Passage 3		Passage 4	
1.	C	12.	A	23.	B	34.	D
2.	B	13.	B	24.	B	35.	A
3.	B	14.	B	25.	D	36.	C
4.	D	15.	B	26.	C	37.	B
5.	D	16.	B	27.	B	38.	C
6.	C	17.	A	28.	A	39.	C
7.	B	18.	C	29.	B	40.	B
8.	D	19.	B	30.	A	41.	A
9.	C	20.	B	31.	A	42.	B
10.	D	21.	D	32.	C	43.	B
11.	A	22.	D	33.	C	44.	C

Topic Areas by Question

Expression of Ideas

Passage 1: Questions 3-4, 6-8, 10

Passage 2: Questions 14-15, 17-18, 21-22

Passage 3, Questions 23, 25-26, 28, 31-32

Passage 4, Questions 35-36, 39, 41, 43-44

Standard English Conventions

Passage 1: Questions 1-2, 5, 9, 11

Passage 2: Questions 12-13, 16, 19-20

Passage 3, Questions 24, 27, 29-30, 33

Passage 4, Questions 34, 37-38, 40, 42

Answer Explanations
Test 6, Pages 136-151

Passage 1, Pages 136-139

1. <u>C</u> is the correct answer.

The sentence that contains the underlined portion should set up a comparison of conditions using the common phrase "easier than," since building a company today is easier "than" it was earlier. Choose C and eliminate A and D (both of which use "then" instead of "than") and B (which uses the superlative, not the comparative form that the sentence requires, and wrongly separates the form of "easy" from the connected transition "than" with a comma).

2. <u>B</u> is the correct answer.

In the sentence, the adjective "optimal" should refer to "options" that "are optimal." Choose B and eliminate A (which wrongly creates a new independent clause within the sentence). C and D both wrongly assume a singular subject for the underlined verb, perhaps mistaking "Google AdWords" for the subject.

3. <u>B</u> is the correct answer.

The underlined sentence transitions from the idea that the Internet makes building a business "easy" to the idea that technologies can also lead to mis-used business resources. Thus, the Internet could logically be responsible for both benefits and problems. Choose B and avoid A (which completely contradicts the writer's earlier ideas). C (factoring the Internet out of business) and D (negative publicity) raise topics that do not appear in this discussion of the benefits and liabilities of Internet-based business.

4. <u>D</u> is the correct answer.

At this point, the writer needs to call attention to a negative trend or chain of events in business: D does so in clear language that avoids distracting informal expressions. In contrast, A, B, and C are all too colloquial for this formal and analytic passage, and some of the words that these answers use (such as "kerfuffle," which means "commotion") do not fit the context of the writer's discussion.

5. D is the correct answer.

The underlined portion should specify what, exactly, "will be formed on questionable premises." Problematic "businesses" could be formed in this manner, so that D is a clear and effective answer. A, B, and C all use ambiguous pronouns that could wrongly refer to the nouns in the previous paragraph, or to some undefined set of ideas.

6. C is the correct answer.

The paragraph discusses the problematic case of an "entrepreneur" in technology who must "oversee the work of various employees." C properly calls attention to the topic of employees within a technology company and thus fits the discussion. A (office space), B (publications), and D (business principles) all mention loosely related issues but do not correctly support the paragraph's focus on hiring and managing workers.

7. B is the correct answer.

In context, an entrepreneur without "technology expertise" would have trouble managing technology company employees. B indicates the proper cause-and-effect relationship. A establishes a contrast (NOT a line of connected reasoning), C indicates similarity, and D indicates alternatives.

8. D is the correct answer.

When combining sentences, use logical transitions and concise, well-coordinated sentence structures. D properly uses a dash to designate a description of the "well-coordinated team" and is thus the best answer. A (awkward "it is"), B (awkward and non-standard "such a team as having"), and C (the similarly problematic "well-coordinating a team") all introduce phrases that pad out the new, combined sentence or jumble its contents.

9. C is the correct answer.

To maintain parallelism, a second -ing form should be put in parallel with "selling ad space." As given in C, "positioning the app" is an appropriate choice. A simply mentions "the app," while B and C feature forms of "position" that are not appropriate to the parallel construction in the manner of "positioning."

10. D is the correct answer.

The previous sentence calls attention to the ability of technology platforms to spread useful information through mentors. Web articles offering "guidance" would be similar as useful resources, so that D is an effective answer. A (correcting mistakes) and C (online publishing) mention technology but not guidance or advice. B mentions entrepreneurship but does not clearly mention the necessary topic of technology.

11. <u>A</u> is the correct answer.

Use a semicolon to separate two independent clauses, such as "The Internet . . . can't . . . save" and "it can . . . alert." A properly uses a semicolon in this manner. B wrongly uses only commas to separate out the clauses (and thus creates a comma splice) while C and D wrongly position the semicolon WITHIN the second independent clause.

Passage 2, Pages 140-143

12. <u>A</u> is the correct answer.

In context, the correspondence was "written" by Frank and should take this past participle to indicate that he was its source. A is the best answer, while B and D wrongly use a simple past tense to indicate that the correspondence ITSELF wrote. C adds an unnecessary transition with "which": do not misread "the non-grammatical "which written" for the relatively long but still acceptable "which was written."

13. <u>B</u> is the correct answer.

The purpose of the school described in the sentence would be to train dogs "for" blind people, who would benefit from owning these animals. Choose B as idiomatically correct. A and D would both indicate physical direction (not the PURPOSE of founding a school), while C, "of," indicates that the blind people ALREADY own the dogs, not that new dogs are being trained "for" these people.

14. <u>B</u> is the correct answer.

Sentence 7 refers to the subject of Frank's "letters," a topic that is first introduced in sentence 5, and explains his reasons for seeking out Eustis's services in more detail than sentence 5 does. B is the correct answer, while the current placement in A would split the discussion of the "dog-training school" in sentences 6 and 8. C and D would both place the topic of Frank's desire for a dog AFTER the explanation that he received a dog, and are thus illogical.

15. <u>B</u> is the correct answer.

The underlined sentence continues the paragraph's discussion of the activities of The Seeing Eye and extends this discussion to the topic of "research." Choose B and eliminate A since the sentence focuses on the "organization" but does NOT specifically mention volunteers. Eliminate C because Eustis and Frank were only a direct topic of the PREVIOUS paragraph, and eliminate D because the NEXT paragraph focuses on the new topic of how Seeing Eye puppies are raised.

16. <u>B</u> is the correct answer.

The underlined portion should describe the action of "People," who bring or "accept" Seeing Eye puppies into home settings. Choose B as fitting the context. A (meaning "to evaluate") is out of context, as are C and D (both meaning to "leave out").

17. <u>A</u> is the correct answer.

Make sure to eliminate redundant phrasing. A effectively presents only new information about the free veterinary care for Seeing Eye puppies. B features redundancy with "complimentary" and "free of charge," C needlessly repeats the idea that the dogs are being "raised," and D features too many similar phrases with "also," "in addition," and "and."

18. <u>C</u> is the correct answer.

In context, the underlined word should describe the action of "Puppy raisers" at "meetings," which these people would naturally "attend." C reflects the proper context. A and B are both overly wordy and describe small physical movements, while D would wrongly indicate that the puppy raisers obtain or receive meetings (much as they would physical items), not that they appear at the meetings.

19. <u>B</u> is the correct answer.

If a descriptive or non-essential phrase between commas is disregarded or deleted, the sentence that contains the phrase should still make grammatical sense. In B, deleting the phrase between commas results in the effective construction "include . . . German shepherds." Choose this answer and eliminate A, which would result in "include . . . to" if the phrase is deleted. C breaks proper colon usage by using a colon AND another transition ("to") to introduce a list, while D breaks the connected phrase "limited to" with a comma.

20. <u>B</u> is the correct answer.

The subject of the sentence consists of three nouns ("Act . . . laws . . . legislation") joined by "and" and is thus plural. Choose B and eliminate A as singular. C and D both turn the sentence into a long fragment by inserting unnecessary transitions.

21. <u>D</u> is the correct answer.

The underlined sentence should indicate WHY some Seeing Eye puppies do not ultimately become guide dogs. To build on this topic, D mentions behavioral and medical issues, and is thus the correct answer. A (breeding practices) and C (number of dogs over a blind person's life) do not mention direct problems with the puppies, while B only mentions dogs that are SUCCESSFUL and thus focuses on a different issue.

22. <u>D</u> is the correct answer.

The underlined transition introduces a sentence about how The Seeing Eye currently "enables" certain benefits. Calling attention to how the organization operates "Today" would be appropriate. Choose D as the best answer, and eliminate A, since the sentence continues the writer's positive tone but does not indicate that The Seeing Eye itself RESPONDS to the writer's own ideas, as set forward in the previous sentence. B and C both indicate contrasts or differences and should thus be eliminated.

Passage 3, Pages 144-147

23. <u>B</u> is the correct answer.

The underlined portion describes "Henry Higgins," a character in a play about "egotism" who could appropriately be described as "self-absorbed." Choose B and eliminate A and C as needlessly colloquial. D can be eliminated for the same reason, and because "pesky" is closer in meaning to "annoying" than to "egotistical."

24. <u>B</u> is the correct answer.

The subject of the underlined verb is the noun series "Intellectualism . . . subtlety . . . fussiness." Thus, the verb should be plural, and should NOT be divided from its subject by a single unit of punctuation. B, "provide.," is the best answer. A and C wrongly split the final noun in the series (which should form a connection) from the verb with a single comma, while C and D both use singular verbs.

25. <u>D</u> is the correct answer.

On the basis of the previous paragraph, Shaw was known for "subtlety" and would thus be unlikely to write a "sensational" script. This is a natural interpretation of his traits, so that D is the best answer. Scholars (A) and Shaw's own words (B) are never mentioned, while the sentence containing the underlined portion describes an expected situation and NOT a reversal or irony (C).

26. <u>C</u> is the correct answer.

In the first paragraph, the writer calls attention to Shaw's perceived "fussiness," a quality that C highlights as questionable or open to dispute. Choose this answer as appropriate to the prompt. A (underestimation), B (implied discomfort), and D (mistaken "core audience") all raise possible negatives, but not negatives that the passage specifically or directly attributes to Shaw at any point.

27. B is the correct answer.

In the portion of the sentence after the colon, what the settings "include" is essential information (since otherwise the sentence would only vaguely refer to "settings" without further details) and should NOT be separated from the main clause with a comma. Choose B and eliminate A for this reason. C (comma splice) and D (two independent clauses without a comma) both commit errors in sentence structure.

28. A is the correct answer.

The phrase "suited to" means "appropriate to" and reflects the idea that a given set facilitates certain types of activities. Choose A as the best, most concise choice for the context. In contrast, B, C, and D are needlessly wordy and colloquial.

29. B is the correct answer.

The subject of the sentence is "Each," which is singular, so choose B as the best answer. A and C both introduce inappropriate plurals (possible if "men" is mistaken as the subject) while D creates a sentence fragment.

30. A is the correct answer.

The underlined portion should be in agreement with "victim," and the victim could be a single "community leader." Choose A and eliminate B and D as faulty plurals. C, "that of," wrongly indicates that the possible victim is some possession or property of a community leader, not the ACTUAL community leader.

31. A is the correct answer.

While sentence 4 introduces Richard and Anthony, sentence 5 explains that they "convinced" of the same possibility. The proposed sentence would effectively introduce a more detailed discussion of their "one opinion in common." Choose A, and eliminate B, C, and D as answers that wrongly place the introduction of the opinion AFTER its clear explanation in sentence 5.

32. C is the correct answer.

The proposed sentence calls attention to "most of Shaw's dramas," a much broader group than the actual focus of the paragraph, *The Devil's Disciple* mainly on its own. Choose C and eliminate A because the new sentence is in fact a distraction from *The Devil's Disciple*. Note that the sentence mainly describes a feature of Shaw's work at large, rather than raising clear negatives about Shaw himself (eliminating B) or Shaw's viewers (eliminating D).

33. C is the correct answer.

It is possible to count quips, or clever sayings, so that the word "number" should be used to refer back to "quips." The word "number" itself is singular, and should be the subject of the underlined verb. C fulfills these conditions, while A and B both use the word "amount" (only appropriate for measurement of quantities that do NOT enable counting) and B and D both use plural verbs.

Passage 4, Pages 148-151

34. <u>D</u> is the correct answer.

The underlined pronoun is part of an imperative sentence ("Imagine") that is addressed to the reader in second person, or to "you." D is thus the appropriate possessive, while A, B, and C are all based on third-person pronouns that cannot refer to a "you" who is being urged to imagine an action.

35. <u>A</u> is the correct answer.

The underlined verb should help to describe the process followed by scientists who made recent discoveries, or who were able to "detect" corrugations. A is appropriate, while B (to give emphasis), C (to aggressively pursue), and D (to think about) do not fit the essential context of making a discovery.

36. <u>C</u> is the correct answer.

For this question, the prompt calls for "new" and "specific" information. C properly explains the "seismic imaging techniques" and relates them to the "oil industry," which is not mentioned elsewhere. Choose this answer and eliminate the others as redundant. A offers vague positives regarding the researchers' technologies, B reiterates the source mentioned earlier in the paragraph, and D for the most part needlessly emphasizes the "collaborative" aspect of the research that is detailed later in the paragraph.

37. <u>B</u> is the correct answer.

In context, the star is what "pinpoints" a location, so that the phrase "star that pinpoints" should be written as one connected idea and should NOT be broken by punctuation. Choose B and eliminate A, C, and D, all of which wrongly insert a comma between "star" and "that."

38. <u>C</u> is the correct answer.

The underlined word should complete the paired phrase begun with "between." In standard usage, "between . . . and" is the only acceptable combination. Choose C and eliminate A, B, and D as automatically breaking a standard idiomatic pairing.

39. <u>C</u> is the correct answer.

While the paragraph and the passage as a whole are both devoted to scientific mapping of geographical features near Costa Rica, the proposed sentence wrongly shifts emphasis to the "tourism industry" in roughly the same area. Choose C and eliminate D (since the proposed content is a distraction, NOT a sentence that would be relevant elsewhere). A and B both wrongly assume that the discussion of tourism directly explains or enhances the discussion of research, rather than introducing an unnecessary outside topic.

40. <u>B</u> is the correct answer.

The underlined pronoun should refer back to "Subduction zones," which are places "where" crust is destroyed. Choose B and eliminate A (which awkwardly indicates that the zones are "in" a situation, not that they ARE a place), C (only appropriate for time), and D (best for introducing a statement).

41. <u>A</u> is the correct answer.

The graph indicates that the Japan and Sumatra tsunamis, taken individually, dealt greater damage than did ALL earthquakes in 2015. This information supports A. Eliminate B (rarely), C (every), and D (always) as answers that indicate broad trends about natural disasters; these are trends that the graph, which simply compares three distinct measures, does not support.

42. <u>B</u> is the correct answer.

The proper phrasing for "hypothetical" causes and effects is the subjunctive "were [cause] . . . would [effect]." Only B properly employs this construction. A uses present tense, B uses future tense, and C uses a past tense.

43. <u>B</u> is the correct answer.

The paragraph presents information about the "changes" and "details" revealed by the imaging, so that B properly calls attention to features or "secrets" that the imaging uncovered. Choose this answer and eliminate A, C, and D, all of which reference FURTHER projects as opposed to continuing the passage's focus on the PRESENT findings involving the imaging.

44. <u>C</u> is the correct answer.

While the sentence that precedes the underlined portion describes changes "in groove direction," the sentence that contains the underlined portion offers a new detail about "rougher areas." Both sentences describe features that the imaging revealed, so that C properly indicates the presentation of additional details. A indicates a contrast, B makes the unjustified assumption that the writer or reader should be surprised, and D would only be appropriate to a second sentence that returned to or intensified major ideas from the first, not to a second sentence that provides related but NEW information.

NOTE: Passage 4, "Undersea Mapping Finds Its Groove," is adapted from "Giant grooves discovered on an earthquake fault offshore Costa Rica." 12 February 2018, U.S. Geological Survey. https://www.usgs.gov/center-news/giant-grooves-discovered-earthquake-fault-offshore-costa-rica. Accessed 21 June 2018.

Test 7

Writing and Language

2018 SAT Practice

Test 7

Writing and Language Test

35 MINUTES, 44 QUESTIONS

Turn to Section 2 of your answer sheet to answer the questions in this section.

Questions 1-11 are based on the following passage.

Neanderthal Creativity

Around the world, cave paintings offer a glimpse of humanity's earliest origins, evidence of culture fifty or more thousand years ago. Experts have always attributed cave painting to modern humans, homo sapiens, even though another hominid, the Neanderthal, is known to have been **1** happening there indubitably.

1

A) NO CHANGE

B) present contemporaneously.

C) right about then.

D) the same thing.

Neanderthals originated in Europe approximately 240,000 years ago and eventually spread throughout central and northern Asia, ultimately going extinct approximately 40,000 years ago. Traditional scholarship has emphasized their differences from **[2]** homo sapiens. For instance, Neanderthals possessed a stockier build with shorter limbs and longer torso, along with other adaptations well suited to a chilly European climate. **[3]** Interactions between homo sapiens and Neanderthals were limited at best. However, Neanderthals' brains were almost as large (when evaluated in relation to body mass) as **[4]** homo sapiens, and new evidence has convinced some researchers that Neanderthals were not the slow-witted, apelike foils to modern humans that they are often depicted as. Perhaps Neanderthals are better classified as a subspecies of humanity **[5]** then as a separate species.

2

Which choice best combines the sentences at the underlined portion?

A) homo sapiens; as Neanderthals had

B) homo sapiens; from

C) homo sapiens, including

D) homo sapiens, despite

3

The writer wishes to include an additional detail that supports the passage's analysis of Neanderthals and homo sapiens. Which choice is most appropriate?

A) NO CHANGE

B) Fossilized Neanderthal remains offer firm evidence in this regard.

C) Homo sapiens, in contrast, originated in a hot savanna climate.

D) Indeed, homo sapiens and Neanderthals differ in several respects.

4

A) NO CHANGE

B) homo sapien's

C) homo sapien's brains

D) homo sapiens' brains

5

A) NO CHANGE

B) than as

C) from

D) to

CONTINUE

Test 7

[1] Archaeologists can use a variety of methods to date cave paintings. [2] For example, **6** if they have an animal as what is depicted in a painting, researchers can look to the local fossil record to see when that animal was present. [3] A potentially more precise dating technique measures the radioactive decay of uranium into thorium, which occurs at a known rate.

[4] If the calcium carbonate deposits are large enough to sample, scientists can measure the amount of uranium that has decayed into thorium. [5] To date cave art by this method, archaeologists must find cave art over which water containing small **7** amounts of uranium and calcium have flowed, gradually creating a calcium carbonate buildup over the painting. [6] From such measurements, they could determine a minimum date for the painting, which must be at least as old as the mineral deposit on top of it. **8**

6
A) NO CHANGE
B) a painting of an animal,
C) if a painting depicts an animal,
D) when there is a painting where an animal is,

7
A) NO CHANGE
B) amounts of uranium and calcium has
C) numbers of uranium and calcium have
D) numbers of uranium and calcium has

8
To make this paragraph most logical, sentence 4 should be placed
A) where it is now.
B) after sentence 1.
C) after sentence 5.
D) after sentence 6.

CONTINUE

Using a highly sensitive version of uranium-thorium dating, a team of archaeologists has dated three cave paintings in Spain to an age of at least **[9]** 65,000 years (or 20,000 years older than the earliest migration of homo sapiens into Europe). If this date is correct, then some cave paintings are the work of Neanderthals. **[10]** Although archaeologists have frequently used the episodes depicted in cave paintings to make inferences about early human societies, these experts would now have evidence that Neanderthals exhibited additional human traits, particularly abstract thought and culture. The findings have been controversial, but as more teams apply this dating technique to more sites, these conclusions may find **[11]** widespread adoption and, researchers may discover Neanderthal inventiveness behind paintings elsewhere in Europe and Asia.

9

A) NO CHANGE

B) 65,000 years, or 20,000 (years older than the earliest migration of homo sapiens

C) 65,000 years, or 20,000 years older than (the earliest migration of homo sapiens

D) 65,000 years, or 20,000 years older than the earliest migration of (homo sapiens

10

Which choice provides the most effective transition from one idea to the next in this paragraph?

A) NO CHANGE

B) Although efforts are being made to assess the Neanderthal cave paintings using additional dating methods,

C) Although archaeologists have long known that Neanderthals used tools and had the capacity for language,

D) Although research regarding cave paintings by humans has seldom led to scholarly dispute,

11

A) NO CHANGE

B) widespread adoption, and researchers

C) widespread adoption; and researchers

D) widespread adoption, and, researchers

CONTINUE

Test 7

Questions 12-22 are based on the following passage.

CRCs Behind the Scenes

Clinical trials allow for scientific innovation to progress safely and efficiently. New biomedical treatments such as drugs and medical devices must be carefully studied **[12]** <u>to determine, whether they are safe and effective at treating the problem</u> that they were designed to solve. By testing these treatments on a small group of human participants, **[13]** <u>data can be collected by specialists</u> to assess the risks and benefits of the treatment before it is made available to the wider population. Clinical research coordinators (CRC) are the professionals charged with overseeing research trials. **[14]** <u>They therefore play an important role in both advancing medical innovation and protecting public safety.</u>

12

A) NO CHANGE

B) to determine whether they are safe and effective, at treating the problem

C) to determine whether they are safe and effective at treating the problem,

D) to determine whether they are safe and effective at treating the problem

13

A) NO CHANGE

B) data collection can be done by specialists

C) specialists can collect data

D) specialists' data can be collected

14

Which choice most effectively concludes the paragraph?

A) NO CHANGE

B) They are members of a profession that is poised for both employment growth and wage growth in the near future.

C) Their education often includes a bachelor's degree in a branch of the life sciences, ideally followed by graduate study.

D) They must consequently possess keen interpersonal skills and psychological insight.

CONTINUE

A clinical trial will typically be designed and led [15] by a researcher known as the principal investigator, or PI. The work of a clinical research coordinator does not usually involve collecting or analyzing scientific data but instead [16] focus on the behind the scenes work that makes it possible for the trial to run.

15

The writer is considering revising the underlined portion to read as follows.

> by a single researcher.

Should the writer make this revision to the passage?

A) Yes, because the new version eliminates redundant phrasing.

B) Yes, because the original version wrongly indicates that a CRC can collect or analyze data.

C) No, because the original version features details that support the writer's argument about the importance of CRCs.

D) No, because the original version introduces a concept that continues to be important to the passage.

16

A) NO CHANGE

B) focuses

C) to focus

D) focused

CONTINUE

Test 7

Long before a trial begins, a clinical research coordinator will begin to take steps to make it possible. For example, once a study has been designed by the principal investigator, it will need to be reviewed by an ethics board to **[17]** ensure, that the rights, safety, and well-being of all participants will be protected during the study. **[18]** The CRC will most likely be the individual to draft the proposal to the ethics board to make a persuasive case for why the planned trial is safe and ethical. **[19]** Although clinical trials are very expensive, they are typically sponsored by either a governmental organization or a private company that provides the necessary funds. CRCs will often be the ones to develop and negotiate a budget for the trial with the sponsor.

17

A) NO CHANGE
B) ensure that
C) ensure, which
D) ensure which

18

At this point, the writer is considering adding the following sentence to the passage.

> A practiced and competent principal investigator can earn an annual salary of $72,000, almost $25,000 more than the median salary for an entry-level CRC.

Should the writer add this content?

A) Yes, because it resolves a point of confusion that the writer acknowledges earlier in the paragraph.
B) Yes, because it further explains the job duties that principal investigators must assume.
C) No, because it provides information irrelevant to the passage's main topic.
D) No, because it draws attention away from the topic of CRC protocols.

19

A) NO CHANGE
B) Unless
C) Since
D) Until

CONTINUE

Once approval and funds have been secured, the role of the CRC typically becomes focused on the [20] individuals where it will participate in the trial as subjects. The CRC will often play an important role in recruiting participants. Such a professional will also create the documents that allow participants to understand the trial and give informed consent. Throughout the trial (which can sometimes run for many years), CRCs perform vital tasks like ensuring that all the data collected are verified and stored [21] in the firmest shape, and guaranteeing patient confidentially. They will often also be the individuals who liaise with the sponsors and keep them up to date on the progress of the trial. The number of participants and duration of a trial will influence [22] the level of challenge and complexity, as a natural impact, in working as a CRC.

20

A) NO CHANGE
B) individuals, they will
C) individuals who will
D) individuals whom will

21

The writer wishes to indicate that work as a CRC involves important responsibilities, and wishes to maintain the tone of the passage. Which choice best accomplishes these goals?

A) NO CHANGE
B) like nobody else can,
C) safely and accurately,
D) with righteousness,

22

A) NO CHANGE
B) the level, measure, and extent of the complex challenge
C) the level of complexity
D) it

CONTINUE

Test 7

Questions 23-33 are based on the following passage and supplementary material.

UX Design: What's the Use?

User experience design, also known as UX design, encompasses all aspects of a human experience as it relates to any type of system or product. It has its roots in the relationships between humans, machines, and their contextual environments, dating back to the 1940s. With the introduction of the personal computer in the 1990s, UX design **23** become more important in order to sell computers. **24** The spending habits of customers have changed substantially, with smaller, sleeker devices finding new prominence in marketing efforts.

See Page 186 for the citation for this text.

23

A) NO CHANGE

B) became

C) becomes

D) will become

24

The writer wishes to call attention to a motivation for the development and popularization of UX design. Which choice best accomplishes this goal?

A) NO CHANGE

B) In the years ahead, the field of UX design may see significant overlap with new developments in marketing-based artificial intelligence.

C) Charting an entire system of interactions was needed to win over the customer in terms of usability, accessibility, and pure pleasure.

D) For many, UX design is a field that thrives on ingenuity; the lack of a discipline-related degree is seldom a barrier for a truly creative designer.

CONTINUE

UX design, while in the retail world embraced primarily by online and interactive companies such as Amazon and Facebook, has become increasingly relevant for other products. Nikkel Blaase, a UX product and interaction designer, states that product thinking is the next big thing in UX design: "Thinking in products means thinking in specific user's problems, in jobs to be done, in goals, and in revenues." [25] Moreover, UX designers themselves take immense personal pride in the products that they create. Designers in this context are creating emotional connections between a product [26] and a user. Innovator Jean-Claude Junqua, who started and developed research and development activities for Panasonic in Silicon Valley and for [27] other companies has noted the decline in brand loyalty and increase in customer power today.

25

The writer is considering deleting the underlined portion. Should this content be kept or deleted?

A) Kept, because it helps to explain the growing prominence of UX design.

B) Kept, because it indicates why UX designers are capable of understanding products from the perspective of consumers.

C) Deleted, because it shifts emphasis away from the paragraph's focus on how designers respond to users.

D) Deleted, because it introduces an idea that experts such as Blaase and Junqua might dispute.

26

A) NO CHANGE

B) from

C) with

D) to

27

A) NO CHANGE

B) other companies, has noted the decline

C) other companies has noted, the decline

D) other companies has noted the decline,

CONTINUE

Test 7

GoPro is a successful consumer product company (famous for making action cameras) that incorporates UX design into all aspects of the firm in order to provide the best user experience. Designers work closely with product managers and are involved in the product definition, concept, and prototyping phases, constantly testing developments with customers. These designers only [28] overwhelm full product development after they have completely validated their concept through customer feedback. The company goes further, having codified "this commitment to UX in a set of design principles" that drive products and services.

To ensure that GoPro's employees understand what makes their customers' experiences enjoyable, the company instituted a "Live it, Eat it, Love it" employee program. Employees are free explore their everyday interests but have to record [29] it using a GoPro, effectively taking on the roles of [30] a GoPro. Vanessa Cho, director of UX at GoPro, states, "We need to make sure we're capturing the undocumented and the unexpected [aspects of using the product]; [31] only then can we maximize—in all respects—our company's profitability."

28

A) NO CHANGE
B) position
C) seize
D) undertake

29

A) NO CHANGE
B) that
C) their activities
D) design principles

30

A) NO CHANGE
B) GoPro consumers.
C) those of a GoPro Consumer.
D) those of GoPro Consumers.

31

Which choice most effectively concludes the discussion in this paragraph?

A) NO CHANGE
B) only then can we recruit the most engaged—and the most innovative—developers working today.
C) only then can we understand what our employees—and our investors—truly value.
D) only then can we deliver useful and usable—and truly delightful—experiences.

CONTINUE

Beyond customer experience, there is evidence that UX investments can enhance corporate performance. A post online in ForbesCommunityVoice states, "Studies show that companies that invest in UX see a lower cost of customer acquisition, lower support cost, **32** superior customer retention rates, and superior increases in market share, according to a study performed by Forrester. When compared to their peers over the past few years, the top 10 companies leading in customer experience **33** were aided by the growth of the S&P Index, exhibiting significantly greater returns."

Value Increase as a Percentage of 2013 Base Price: S&P 500 and Groups of 10 Companies (Weighted by Market Cap)

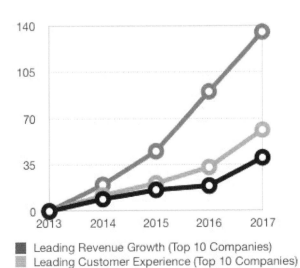

32

The following table presents the results of a 2016 study of four companies that invested heavily in UX design and four that did not.

Percent Growth from 2012-2013

	UX-Heavy	UX-Light	Difference
same-store sales	4%	12%	8%
total profit	21%	22%	1%
market share	20%	5%	15%
customer retention	42%	33%	9%

Which choice presents the most accurate reading of the table?

A) NO CHANGE

B) superior customer retention rates, and superior increases in profitability,

C) and increased customer retention, but see decreases in profitability,

D) and increased market share, but see decreases in profitability,

33

Which choice presents the most accurate interpretation of the data comparing the groups of companies to the S&P Index?

A) NO CHANGE

B) were aided by the relative weakness of

C) consistently outperformed

D) at times underperformed

CONTINUE

Test 7

Questions 34-44 are based on the following passage.

Stellavie's Universe of Printmaking Possibilities

The best home decoration manages to say something original about its owners, [34] without making a big deal of small things. In this regard, the Hamburg-based printmaking firm Stellavie deserves the highest praise: Stellavie prints can blend in with various furnishings [35] without giving any guests with the good taste to notice them something to talk about. At present, Stellavie offers a few distinct series groups—the Star Map prints, the Exceptionally Great Espresso prints, and the recent Movie Director Portrait prints— [36] all of them are executed in two colors. Those two-color combinations include gold on black, gold on emerald green, and white on blue.

34

A) NO CHANGE
B) without having people get too put-out.
C) without calling undue attention to itself.
D) without an ostentatious mind.

35

A) NO CHANGE
B) while
C) unless
D) by

36

A) NO CHANGE
B) all of which
C) all of whom
D) all

CONTINUE

Stellavie is owned and operated by Steffen Heidemann and Viktoria Klein, who have persisted with **37** a unified and functional, as well as minimalistic aesthetic that is only positioned to grow in popularity in the years to come. Even now, artistically executed maps, infographics, and diagrams **38** enlarge in fashionable apartments. After developing the star maps and espresso guides in an array of colors, Steffen and Viktoria partnered with illustrator Julian Rentzsch to develop portraits of individual filmmakers, which **39** includes a montage-style image of Alfred Hitchcock, David Lynch, Martin Scorsese, Tim Burton, Quentin Tarantino, and Stanley Kubrick. Conceivably, the series could eventually feature Paul Thomas Anderson, Orson Welles, and a variety of other film virtuosos.

37

A) NO CHANGE

B) a unified, functional, and minimalistic

C) a unified, functional, as well as minimalistic

D) a unified—functional, and minimalistic too

38

A) NO CHANGE

B) surge

C) rise up

D) proliferate

39

A) NO CHANGE

B) includes montage-style images

C) include a montage-style image

D) include montage-style images

CONTINUE

In a few short sweeps, each filmmaker portrait combines the visage of a celebrated director with images from one of his or her most famous films. Along the lower portions of the print **40** runs a list of life events and major accomplishments, cleverly formatted in the fonts and styles usually reserved for film credits. "Clever" is also the right description for the glow-in-the-dark and science fiction-inspired "Home Is Where Your Heart Is" print that Steffen and Viktoria have devised. **41**

40

A) NO CHANGE

B) run

C) will run

D) ran

41

Which choice provides the most appropriate concluding statement for the paragraph?

A) This entry represents a movement away from some of Stellavie's earlier devices and towards a style that may appeal more to families with small children.

B) Like the filmmaker portraits, this work ingeniously combines smaller discrete images (spaceships and planets, in this case) into a coherent composition.

C) Though the figures and colors here can seem stark and simple, Stellavie has actually approached the idea of "home" with a touch of melancholy irony.

D) Rich in color and dynamic shape, this recent print may not prove as easily adaptable to a range of home settings as some of Stellavie's more "minimalistic" works.

CONTINUE

[1] Delightful though all these are, **42** they're a marriage of art and functionality that defines Stellavie. [2] For the alluring star maps, images of both the Northern and the Southern Sky are available and beg to be paired off. [3] A Stellavie espresso diagram is ideally suited to a home office or a kitchen, somewhere busy with real life implements and activity to complement its busy array of illustrations. [4] Such astronomical images are great for transforming a long and formerly empty stretch of wall into a space for contemplation. [5] Viewers can also engage the information present in each series, perhaps by comparing and contrasting constellations from the different hemispheres, **43** or by considering the possibilities for Stellavie's future printmaking projects. [6] Both cerebral and functional, all Stellavie prints inspire reflection. **44**

42

A) NO CHANGE

B) their's

C) its'

D) it's

43

Which choice effectively offers new information that supports the main idea of the sentence?

A) NO CHANGE

B) or by weighing the decorative potential of the different color schemes available.

C) or by mulling over the distinctions between varieties of espresso beans.

D) or by delving into the influence of ancient mythology on astronomical theories.

44

To make the paragraph most logical, sentence 4 should be placed

A) where it is now.

B) after sentence 1.

C) after sentence 2.

D) after sentence 6.

STOP

If you finish before time is called, you may check your work on this section only.
Do not turn to any other section.

Answer Key: Test 7

Passage 1		Passage 2		Passage 3		Passage 4	
1.	B	12.	D	23.	B	34.	C
2.	C	13.	C	24.	C	35.	B
3.	C	14.	A	25.	C	36.	B
4.	D	15.	D	26.	A	37.	B
5.	B	16.	B	27.	B	38.	D
6.	C	17.	B	28.	D	39.	D
7.	B	18.	D	29.	C	40.	A
8.	C	19.	C	30.	B	41.	B
9.	A	20.	C	31.	D	42.	D
10.	C	21.	C	32.	A	43.	C
11.	B	22.	C	33.	C	44.	C

Topic Areas by Question

Expression of Ideas

Passage 1: Questions 1-3, 6, 8, 10

Passage 2: Questions 14-15, 18-19, 21-22

Passage 3, Questions 24-25, 28, 31-33

Passage 4, Questions 34-35, 38, 41, 43-44

Standard English Conventions

Passage 1: Questions 4-5, 7, 9, 11

Passage 2: Questions 12-13, 16-17, 20

Passage 3, Questions 23, 26-27, 29-30

Passage 4, Questions 36-37, 39, 40, 42

Answer Explanations
Test 7, Pages 162-177

Passage 1, Pages 162-165

1. <u>B</u> is the correct answer.

In context, the writer is describing two organisms (homo sapiens and Neanderthals) which were "present" contemporaneously or at the same time. Choose B as an appropriate phrasing and eliminate A (which describes the Neanderthal as an EVENT that would be happening), C (which is too informal), and D (which wrongly indicates that humans and Neanderthals are IDENTICAL, not similar in a few respects).

2. <u>C</u> is the correct answer.

The combined sentence should call attention to specific "differences" between Neanderthals and homo sapiens, and these differences would "include" features of anatomy and adaptation as described in the sentence's later portions. Choose C and eliminate A and B (each of which wrongly places a fragment after a semicolon). D wrongly indicates a contrast, not a presentation of further details.

3. <u>C</u> is the correct answer.

At this point in the passage, the writer is explaining the "differences" between Neanderthals and homo sapiens. Pointing out that these organisms inhabited different climates, as in C, would continue the writer's analysis. Choose this answer and eliminate A (interactions) and B (fossils) as answers that do not directly continue the discussion of differences. D notes that Neanderthals and homo sapiens were different, but does not provide meaningful additional information.

4. <u>D</u> is the correct answer.

The sentence should compare the brains of Neanderthals to the brains of "homo sapiens," which can be written as a plural possessive as "homo sapiens'." D is thus the best answer. A wrongly compares Neanderthal brains to homo sapiens (the full organisms), while B and C both feature possessives that would indicate a SINGULAR homo sapien and thus break the needed comparison.

5. <u>B</u> is the correct answer.

In the sentence, the standard phrase for comparing two ideas of what Neanderthals are classified "as" is "better . . . than." B is correct, while A mistakes "then" for "than." C and D both feature prepositions that break both the standard phrase and the needed parallelism involving "as."

6. <u>C</u> is the correct answer.

The underlined portion should present a condition ("if") that would enable researchers to make a specific type of inquiry. C is appropriate phrasing for a condition, and avoids the wordy, awkward constructions of A and D. B, which simply notes "a painting," does not feature a transition that properly sets up a condition.

7. <u>B</u> is the correct answer.

As mentioned in the sentence, "uranium and calcium" are substances that can be measured but not (like grouped items) counted. The word "amounts" is appropriate for this context, but is NOT the subject of the underlined verb, which should refer to the "water" that "has flowed." B is the best answer, while A and C wrongly use plural verbs and C and D wrongly use the word "numbers," which is only appropriate to items that can be counted.

8. <u>C</u> is the correct answer.

While sentence 5 explains that scientists must find calcium carbonate buildup, sentence 4 explains how scientists can analyze such buildup AFTER it has been found. C thus effectively places sentence 4 after sentence 5, while A reverses the appropriate order. B would split a discussion that surveys different methods with analysis of ONE method, while D would wrongly place an explanation of how the scientists perform analysis AFTER an explanation of a final finding that the analysis could yield.

9. <u>A</u> is the correct answer.

As a unit of punctuation, a parenthesis should help to set off a complete explanatory or qualifying phrase, and should NOT disrupt closely linked idiomatic expressions. A, which sets aside the full idea that 60,000 years can also be understood as 20,000 years older than a specific migration, is the best choice. B wrongly splits "20,000 years," C wrongly splits a linked comparison in "than . . . migration," and D wrongly splits "of homo sapiens."

10. <u>C</u> is the correct answer.

The sentence explains that the Neanderthals are now known to have "additional human traits," so that content describing previously-known human traits such as tool usage and language usage would be appropriate.

Choose C and eliminate both A and D, which focus on humans but NOT on Neanderthals. B mentions "dating methods, a topic of the previous paragraph, yet this paragraph mostly focuses on Neanderthal traits at the underlined portion and does not mention "additional" methods beyond the one used by the research team.

11. <u>B</u> is the correct answer.

As a conjunction, "and" can be preceded by a comma (NOT a semicolon) when it introduces a clause, but cannot be split from the clause that it introduces by a single comma. Choose B as an effectively-punctuated choice. A and D split "and" from the clause "researchers may discover" with a single comma, while C wrongly places a semicolon before "and."

Passage 2, Pages 166-169

12. <u>D</u> is the correct answer.

The underlined phrase features a series of essential and closely-connected ideas that explain the purpose of studying new treatments, and thus should NOT be split up by commas. Choose D and eliminate A (splitting "determine whether"), B (splitting "effective at"), and C (splitting "problem that").

13. <u>C</u> is the correct answer.

The underlined portion should describe people, who would naturally be "testing" treatments. C properly indicates that "specialists" are responsible for testing, while A, B, and D create misplaced modifies, since "data" and "data collection" cannot perform tests.

14. <u>A</u> is the correct answer.

In the paragraph, the activities of CRCs are linked to "scientific innovation" and to assessment of "risks and benefits." Mentioning both innovation and safety properly reflects this content. Choose A and eliminate B (growth of the profession), C (education), and D (interpersonal and psychological aptitudes), all of which raise topics related the career overall but NOT mentioned specifically in the paragraph.

15. <u>D</u> is the correct answer.

The original version introduces and explains the leadership position of a "principal investigator," which is given additional attention in the paragraph that follows. Choose D and eliminate A, since the writer is explaining the concept for the first time. However, the original version simply indicates that the PR occupies a design and leadership position; it does not provide detail about how or whether this specialist collects data (eliminating B) or support a positive general argument about CRCs (eliminating C).

16. <u>B</u> is the correct answer.

The subject of the underlined verb is "work," which is singular; moreover, the underlined verb should be in parallel with the singular present-tense verb "does . . . involve." B is an effective singular present tense. A is plural, C is out of parallel ("to"), and D breaks agreement of tenses with a past tense.

17. <u>B</u> is the correct answer.

The correct idiomatic phrase for making sure of certain events or qualities is to "ensure that," and this linked idea should introduce a clause WITHOUT itself being separated by a comma. B is the best answer. A wrongly inserts a comma, while C and D wrongly pair "ensure" with the pronoun "which."

18. <u>D</u> is the correct answer.

While the paragraph describes the job duties of a CRC, the proposed content wrongly shifts to a new topic by describing CRC salary figures. D is the best choice, while the fact that the information is a distraction from the paragraph's analysis should be used to eliminate A and B. C uses faulty logic, because the salary figures, though not relevant to the paragraph, ARE potentially relevant to the main topic of a CRC career.

19. <u>C</u> is the correct answer.

The sentence should describe a cause-and-effect relationship, in which "expensive" trials are met with "necessary funds" in response. C is an appropriate choice, while A wrongly sets up a contrast and B and D both indicate hypothetical conditions that may or may not be met, not a challenge that is "typically" met with funding and sponsorship.

20. <u>C</u> is the correct answer.

The underlined phrase should create a reference to "individuals," in this case people "who will" participate. C is the best answer, while A both refers to place ("where") and features the unnecessary pronoun "it." B creates a comma splice while D, "whom," is an object pronoun and CANNOT refer to "individuals" who perform an action as presented in the sentence.

21. <u>C</u> is the correct answer.

The passage indicates that a CRC performs "vital tasks" in terms of data collection, and ministers to patient needs. C properly reflects the passage's positive tone and formal style. The other answers, particularly B, are more informal and refer to inappropriate contexts, such as appearance (A) and morality (D).

22. <u>C</u> is the correct answer.

This question requires the elimination of redundant wording and concepts, which appear in A ("influence," "impact") and B ("level, measure, and extent"). Though concise, D features an ambiguous pronoun that could refer to any one of the singular nouns in the sentence, or to some undefined quality. However, C correctly and clearly explains that the "level of complexity" is being considered in CRC work.

Passage 3, Pages 170-173

23. <u>B</u> is the correct answer.

The underlined verb should refer to the singular "UX design," and should be in past tense since the writer is describing events from the 1990s. B is an appropriate answer, while A is plural, C is present tense, and D is future tense.

24. <u>C</u> is the correct answer.

In the underlined portion, the writer should refer directly to the nature of "UX design" and to the important factors that it has taken into consideration as it has grown in popularity. C references various important elements of a user's experience, while trap answer A refers to customers and to how devices are marketed, but does NOT clearly raise the topic of how consumers use devices. B ("years ahead") refers to the future of UX design, while D (UX designer qualifications) does not explain why the field ITSELF has become popular.

25. <u>C</u> is the correct answer.

While the paragraph mostly discusses how UX designers respond to the needs of users, the underlined sentence focuses on the different topic of how UX designers feel about their own work. Choose C to eliminate this content, and eliminate A and B as overstating the relevance of this information to the writer's analysis of UX design as consumer-oriented. However, there is no reason to believe that UX designers themselves would disagree with the positive statement contained in the sentence, so that D uses faulty logic.

26. <u>A</u> is the correct answer.

When used to pair off two items, "between" should automatically form a paired phrase with "and." A properly features this usage, while B, C, and D feature prepositions that imply range or direction, and that are AUTOMATICALLY incorrect according to standard English usage.

27. <u>B</u> is the correct answer.

The underlined singular verb "has noted" should refer back to "Jean-Claude Junqua" as its subject, and any interrupting phrase should be set off by two units of punctuation or by none at all. B correctly features two commas, while A and C wrongly split the subject and verb with only one comma. D wrongly splits the connected and essential idea "decline in brand loyalty" with a comma.

28. <u>D</u> is the correct answer.

The underlined verb should describe what the designers do to create a product after their ideas have been "validated." These designers would naturally initiate or "undertake" actual development. Choose D and eliminate A as negative, then eliminate B and C as referring to physical movement, not to starting a process.

29. <u>C</u> is the correct answer.

The underlined pronoun should refer to what employees would "record," a noun similar to "everyday interests." C, which references activities, is an appropriate choice. A and B both present ambiguous pronouns that could refer to earlier nouns such as "company" or "program," while D would introduce a noun that has nothing to do with the expected activities of the everyday GoPro users who act much like the employees.

30. <u>B</u> is the correct answer.

The underlined portion should compare the "Employees" mentioned earlier to other people, or to "GoPro consumers." B is an effective choice. A wrongly compares the employees to a GoPro device, while C and D both introduce the unclear pronoun "those" as the items to which the "Employees" are compared.

31. <u>D</u> is the correct answer.

The paragraph as a whole is about employees who use GoPro cameras themselves to understand how consumers might use and enjoy the products, so that D is the best choice and reflects the goal of the employees' work. A (profitability), B (hiring) and C (investors) all refer to elements of running a business but do not address the central topic of understanding the users' experiences.

32. <u>A</u> is the correct answer.

The table indicates that UX-heavy companies are superior to UX-light companies in market share increases and customer retention increases, but inferior in terms of same-store sales increases and total profit increases. Choose A and eliminate B, which uses the wrong profit comparison. C and D both wrongly indicate that UX-heavy companies see DECREASES in profits, not LOWER profit increases.

33. <u>C</u> is the correct answer.

According to the graph, the top companies in customer experience (light gray) ALWAYS performed better than the S&P Index (black). Choose C and eliminate D for this reason. Note that the graph does not in any way indicate the REASONS for this outperformance, as answers A and B do. Thus, eliminate these choices as involving unsupported interpretations of the evidence

Passage 4, Pages 174-177

34. C is the correct answer.

In context, the writer is describing Stellavie's home decorations, which "blend in." Such decoration does not call "undue attention to itself," so that C is an appropriate phrasing. A and B are inappropriately informal, while D calls attention to the wrong context ("mind" or thinking) for home decorations themselves.

35. B is the correct answer.

The "prints" described in the sentence simultaneously blend in and inspire conversation, so that "while" would properly indicate simultaneity. Choose B and eliminate A and C, which both indicate exceptions rather than properties that work together. D would be appropriate for a cause-and-effect relationship, not for TWO qualities that exist at once.

36. B is the correct answer.

To avoid a sentence that wrongly mixes together two independent clauses, the pronoun "which" should be used to refer back to "groups." Choose B and eliminate A and D, each of which wrongly creates a new independent clause after the second dash. C, "whom," features a pronoun that can only refer to people, NOT to groups of things.

37. B is the correct answer.

The most concise and conventional phrasing for a three-item list is "[ITEM 1], [ITEM 2], and [ITEM 3]," a structure that is used properly in B. Choose this option and eliminate A and D (which bring in too many words indicating addition). C wrongly substitutes the wordy "as well as" for the more standard "and."

38. D is the correct answer.

In context, the underlined word describes a trend that appears ready to grow in popularity: more of specific decoration types that are being bought in large numbers or that "proliferate" now may be bought in the future. D fits the context of large numbers and popularity, while A indicates that INDIVIDUAL items are growing larger. B (a sudden increase in energy) and C (a change in physical position) also loosely relate to the concept of increase but do not fit the specific situation.

39. D is the correct answer.

The underlined portion should refer back to several "portraits," which since they are devoted to various "individual filmmakers" would include multiple "images." D uses both the correct plural verb and the correct plural noun. A and B wrongly use singular verbs, while A and C wrongly use singular nouns.

40. <u>A</u> is the correct answer.

The underlined verb takes the inverted subject "list" and is thus singular, and should be in present tense to agree with the other verbs that describe the print. A is thus correct, while B is plural, C is future tense, and D is past tense.

41. <u>B</u> is the correct answer.

The paragraph describes two works from Stellavie, a typical filmmaker portrait and the "Home Is Where Your Heart Is" print, and characterizes each work as clever. B mentions both works and appropriately continues the positive tone. A and C both avoid the important topic of the filmmaker portraits, while D is wrongly critical of the "Home Is Where Your Heart Is" print.

42. <u>D</u> is the correct answer.

The underlined word should refer to the "marriage" (it) that is what defines Stellavie. D offers the proper contraction of "it is," while A and B are both plural and C presents a nonexistent form.

43. <u>C</u> is the correct answer.

The sentence calls attention to the idea that viewers can "engage the information" in Stellavie's constellation series (which is mentioned at length) and espresso series (which could be given additional attention). C refers to information that would naturally be present in the espresso diagrams. Choose this answer and eliminate A (future projects), B (color schemes), and D (astronomical theories, NOT astronomical diagrams). These answers loosely relate to the printmaking and chosen topics of Stellavie but do not mention types of "information" that would be present in the prints described.

44. <u>C</u> is the correct answer.

While sentence 2 refers to the "alluring star maps," sentence 4 refers back to "Such astronomical images" and would thus logically follow sentence 2. Choose C and eliminate A, since sentence 3 only refers to the espresso diagrams. Sentences 1 and 6 refer to Stellavie's projects at large, NOT specifically to the astronomical images as demanded by sentence 4, so that B and D should both be eliminated.

NOTE: Passage 3, "UX Design: What's The Use?," is an adapted excerpt from "Industrial Design: A Competitive Edge for U.S. Manufacturing Success in the Global Economy," Page 19, April 2017, National Endowment for the Arts. https://www.arts.gov/sites/default/files/Industrial-Design-Report-May2017-rev3.pdf. Accessed 21 June 2018.

Test 8

Writing and Language

2018 SAT Practice

Test 8

Writing and Language Test

35 MINUTES, 44 QUESTIONS

Turn to Section 2 of your answer sheet to answer the questions in this section.

Questions 1-11 are based on the following passage and supplementary material.

Rescuing the Hudson River

The Hudson River extends for 315 miles from north to south. It originates in the Adirondack Mountains of Upstate New York, and runs mainly through eastern New York State. The river flows through the Hudson Valley and then drains into the Atlantic Ocean in an area between New York City **[1]** from Jersey City. It is not

1
A) NO CHANGE
B) and
C) to
D) or

just a river; it is also a tidal estuary where salty ocean waters meet with freshwater that runs from the land. As a diverse ecosystem, the Hudson River exhibits a unique [2] matching of conditions in the natural world. This area is the natural habitat of fish, wildlife, birds, large crustaceans, zoo-plankton, plants, and phytoplankton.

Between 1947 and 1977, the General Electric Company, a global industrial giant, polluted the Hudson River by dispensing [3] chemical toxins, them being polychlorinated biphenyls also known as PCBs. This group of man-made chemicals can be in liquid or solid form; in the colors that they exhibit, these substances range from taking on an oily and clear appearance [4] to substances that display yellow hues. They have no smell or taste, and are very resistant to pressure and extreme temperatures. [5] There is no known natural source of PCBs in the environment.

2

A) NO CHANGE
B) agreement
C) bunch
D) set

3

A) NO CHANGE
B) chemical toxins—polychlorinated biphenyls
C) chemical toxins; polychlorinated biphenyls
D) chemical toxins polychlorinated biphenyls

4

A) NO CHANGE
B) to when they have yellow hues.
C) to displaying yellow hues.
D) to yellow in hue.

5

Which choice would best support the claim that the pollution can be traced to General Electric?

A) NO CHANGE
B) The potency of PCBs makes their removal from the environment especially complicated.
C) PCBs often inflict completely unintended harm on vulnerable ecosystems.
D) Many different PCBs have been studied by chemical engineers since the 1950s.

CONTINUE

189

[6] It is estimated that at least 10 million pounds of non-toxic runoff were discharged into the waterway from the General Electric's Fort Edward and Hudson Falls capacitor plants. When the PCBs entered the Hudson River, they **[7]** were mixed and deposited at many areas of the river bottom and along the floodplain's shoreline. The Fort Edward and Hudson Falls facilities have since been closed.

General Electric paid for a cleanup of the Upper Hudson to remove over 2.5 million cubic yards of sediment from the river, encompassing a roughly 40-mile stretch from the Troy Dam to Fort Edward. The progress of this cleanup is assessed every five years. However, its success has been a subject of controversy.

6

Which choice provides an interpretation of the information from the chart that is most relevant to the writer's discussion?

A) NO CHANGE

B) It is estimated that roughly 8 million pounds of toxic runoff in total

C) It is estimated that roughly 3 million pounds of PCBs, dioxin, and furan

D) It is estimated that 1.5 million pounds of various kinds of PCBs

7

A) NO CHANGE

B) were mixed, combined, and deposited

C) were mixed, left, and variously settled

D) were mixed, deposited, and then left

Industrial Runoff, Fort Edwards and Hudson Falls Plants (1947-1977)

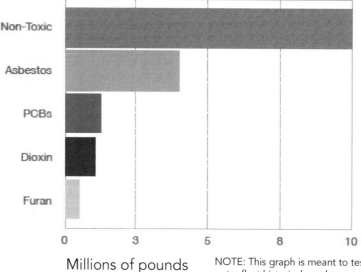

Millions of pounds

NOTE: This graph is meant to test critical thinking skills and may not reflect historical numbers.

CONTINUE

PCBs were known to cause harmful effects to people who ate fish from the river or drank the water. The National Institute for Occupational Safety and Healthy identified them as a potential carcinogen in the workplace, and the National Toxicology Program has reported that they are likely to cause cancer. PCBs also afflicted all of the local wildlife dependent on the river for food. **8** Important people said it was about time to ban them in the United States in 1979.

Cleaning up the Hudson River has been a complicated process and renewal is considered a long-term project. Two hundred miles of the river are classified by the Environmental Protection Agency (EPA) **9** for a Superfund site, one of the largest in the United States. The EPA's Superfund program cleans up some of the most contaminated lands in an effort to protect the health of the public and the environment. **10** The dumping of PCBs in the Hudson River **11** will reveal the detrimental effects of pollution on individuals, businesses, and communities.

8

A) NO CHANGE
B) They were banned from use
C) Their banning was now there
D) They weren't happening

9

A) NO CHANGE
B) with
C) at
D) as

10

At this point, the writer is considering inserting the following sentence.

> After all, ingesting PCB-contaminated material can lead to health problems.

Should the writer insert this content here?

A) Yes, because it addresses a counter-argument.
B) Yes, because it re-states the writer's thesis.
C) No, because it places too much emphasis on a minor topic.
D) No, because it mostly repeats information from elsewhere in the passage.

11

A) NO CHANGE
B) revealing
C) reveals
D) reveal

CONTINUE

Test 8

Questions 12-22 are based on the following passage.

Tango for All: A Visit to the Dardo Galletto Studios

[12] Unlike other forms of dance, tango has shaped the style and content of recent film. Even if you've never been to a live tango performance, you have probably seen pop culture testaments to the dance's image of passion and sophistication (such as the film *Scent of a Woman*) or send-ups of that image (such as the film *Some Like It Hot*). At the Dardo Galletto Studios in Midtown Manhattan, [13] they can see something very [14] different: such as tango as a form of calculated, concentrated artistry.

12

Which choice serves as the best introduction to the paragraph?

A) NO CHANGE

B) In recent years, tango has seen a resurgence in popularity across media.

C) As a form of dance, tango is famous for its air of romance and vibrancy.

D) Tango experts are increasingly committed to making tango more accessible.

13

A) NO CHANGE

B) one can

C) you can

D) he or she can

14

A) NO CHANGE

B) different, such as: tango

C) different: that is tango

D) different: tango

CONTINUE

[1] Take the elevator to the 11th-floor Dardo Galletto dance hall around 10:00 or 11:00, and you'll discover an appreciative, easygoing assembly of professional dancers, enthusiastic novices, and dance enthusiasts. [2] In 2015, for instance, renowned Argentine tangoists Gabriel Missé and Analía Centurión performed nighttime dance sets and offered tango lessons at the Studios. [3] Though designed as displays of technical prowess, these performances weren't dry or academic. [4] Rather, 15 which were central to the festive and welcoming atmosphere that reigns, even now, on any given evening. [5] If you had had the privilege of watching a showcase by Missé and Centurión, 16 you witness a tango that uses bracing, staccato footwork to hold your attention. 17

Each Missé and Centurión performance was prefaced by an open-to-the-public session of the milonga. Traditionally, the milonga is associated with fast movement and with underworld nightclubs. The Dardo Galletto version, 18 accordingly, was considerably toned-down.

15

A) NO CHANGE
B) they were
C) those of them were
D) DELETE the underlined portion.

16

A) NO CHANGE
B) you are witnessing
C) you will be witnessing
D) you would have witnessed

17

To make the order of ideas in the paragraph most logical, sentence 1 should be placed

A) where it is now.
B) after sentence 2.
C) after sentence 4.
D) after sentence 5.

18

A) NO CHANGE
B) unmistakably,
C) in contrast,
D) as noted,

CONTINUE

Test 8

These milonga sessions [19] cohered amateurs, semi-professionals, and everyone in between, a format which only added to the charm. Indeed, it is heartening to see novices and virtuosos side-by-side. In a few cases, milonga veterans showed newcomers to the Dardo Galletto Studios the rudiments of the dance.

Normally, Missé and Centurión [20] would only take the floor after two or three hours. The wait was worth it, and not just because that wait involved complimentary snacks and an arresting 11th-floor view. Though Missé and [21] Centurión sometimes went, spinning from one end of the Dardo Galletto floor to the other, their dancing relies on fast movement and assured precision. Viewers had the thrill of watching Missé fire his legs across the floor (and, sometimes, straight between Centurión's feet) at high velocity.

19

A) NO CHANGE
B) equated
C) made into one
D) brought together

20

Which of the following choices best maintains the tone and style of the writer's discussion?

A) NO CHANGE
B) didn't make a big deal of getting on the floor for a while.
C) were not all that interested in getting on the floor until two or three hours were done.
D) refrained scrupulously from assuming the floor.

21

A) NO CHANGE
B) Centurión, sometimes went spinning from one end of the Dardo Galletto floor
C) Centurión sometimes went spinning from one end of the Dardo Galletto floor,
D) Centurión sometimes went spinning from one end of the Dardo Galletto floor

CONTINUE

In a pleasantly surprising move, Missé and Centurión also showed how well-suited their style is to a very different kind of music: classic rock-and-roll. Watching them dance to "Blue Suede Shoes" was not only a treat, **22** but it also served as a reference to the classical training that explains much of their renown. Anyone who witnesses Missé's take on "Blue Suede Shoes" will realize that much of his dancing—in tango and beyond—is guided by jauntiness and playfulness.

Which choice best supports the writer's discussion of Missé and Centurión at this point in the passage?

A) NO CHANGE

B) but it was also a fine demonstration of what makes them supremely entertaining as tangoists.

C) but it also called attention to the fundamental similarities between tango and other forms of dance prominent in popular culture.

D) but it also served as a reference point for visitors unfamiliar with the tango and the milonga.

CONTINUE

Test 8

Questions 23-33 are based on the following passage.

The Professional Possibilities of Geomatics

Geomatics is a field of study that involves using a range of mapping technologies to document and examine features of the earth's surface. Geomatics originated with the practice of land surveying, [23] <u>which has existed since in ancient times and which contemporary geomatics has adapted to 21st-century technology.</u> The modern practice involves recording the position of specific points or features (for example, a hill or river), often with the aim of establishing boundaries and divisions. The rise of geomatics as a field [24] <u>coincides with</u> advancements in technology that made capturing and storing data about the earth's surface not only more sophisticated, but also more complex. As a result, modern geomatics is a [25] <u>discipline, that combines innovative technology</u> with the investigation of the natural world.

23

The writer is considering revising the underlined portion to read as follows.

which has existed since ancient times.

Should the writer make this revision?

A) Yes, because the new version omits ideas that are made evident elsewhere in the paragraph.

B) Yes, because the new version eliminates a point of confusion about 21st-century geomatics.

C) No, because the advancement of geomatics technology is the paragraph's primary topic.

D) No, because the writer's definition of "ancient times" would consequently become unclear.

24

A) NO CHANGE

B) collaborates with

C) is the same as

D) goes to

25

A) NO CHANGE

B) discipline that combines innovative technology,

C) discipline that combines innovative technology

D) discipline, that combines innovative technology,

CONTINUE

[26] <u>When you study geomatics, you</u> will typically be introduced to concepts from geography, land-surveying, and cartography (the study of maps). GIS and remote sensing are two technical areas which geomatics uses heavily, and which would also usually be studied. A GIS, or a "geographic information system," is a digital tool used to analyze and model spatial data. "Remote sensing" [27] <u>will refer</u> to the practice of using a sensor to gain information about an object (for example, a buried rock) without having to make physical contact with that object.

[26]

A) NO CHANGE
B) Someone who has chosen to study geomatics
C) People who have chosen, decisively, that they are going to study geomatics
D) With the study of geomatics, if one chooses it one

[27]

A) NO CHANGE
B) refers
C) had referred
D) is referring

CONTINUE

28 [Until] geomatics involves being able to understand and analyze geospatial data (not just collect it), knowledge of statistics, data analysis, and programming may also be useful. While the activities specialists in these areas can take place in conjunction with a project in industry, **29** [such as scouting an unpopulated area with new optical devices] or assessing the presence of resources, **30** [it is] often applied to support sustainability or conservation efforts. Students who plan to use their geomatics education in this way may benefit from studying the theory and philosophy of sustainability.

28

A) NO CHANGE

B) Where

C) Because

D) Although

29

Which choice would offer a supporting detail that most effectively relates to the writer's discussion?

A) NO CHANGE

B) such as determining the safety of building a structure

C) such as developing software based on data collected through fieldwork

D) such as mapping the quickest route through a difficult topography

30

A) NO CHANGE

B) they are

C) the discipline of geomatics is

D) specialists in geomatics are

CONTINUE

[1] Geomatics prepares individuals for a wide range of related careers. [2] Many natural resource fields—including geology, forestry, and pursuits connected to [31] fisheries, hire individuals with geomatics knowledge to contribute to work like forest fire prevention, resource exploration, earthquake monitoring, and quota selection. [3] Graduates may also find work in environmental monitoring such as performing environmental impact assessments and pollution control. [4] Otherwise, graduates who loved studying the technical aspects of their degree may be [32] drew to careers in spatial data management or software development. [5] Closely-related applications include ecological research modeling and studying data related to climate change and habitat. [6] By working as, for example, a geospatial software engineer, someone with a geomatics background could help to create the tools that make it possible for geomatics to remain a cutting-edge field of study. [33]

31

A) NO CHANGE
B) fisheries—hire individuals
C) fisheries, hire individuals—
D) fisheries hire individuals

32

A) NO CHANGE
B) drawn to
C) drew by
D) drawn by

33

To make the paragraph most logical, sentence 5 should be placed

A) where it is now.
B) after sentence 1.
C) after sentence 3.
D) after sentence 6.

CONTINUE

Test 8

Questions 34-44 are based on the following passage and supplementary material.

Acid Rain: What Vehicle Is the Solution?

Most rain that fell before the Industrial Revolution was relatively neutral in pH (i.e. not acidic or basic). Because most organisms aren't equipped to live in acidic or basic surroundings, [34] acid rain has recently re-emerged as a subject of controversy. Post-industrial rain has become [35] increasing, acidic as a result of compounds emitted by factories, cars, and other manmade sources.

Carbon dioxide (CO_2), sulfur dioxide (SO_2) and nitrogen oxides (NO_x) are the main drivers of acid rain because they mix with rainwater to produce acids such as carbonic acid, sulfuric acid, and nitric acid. This acid then damages soil and water systems, as well as the organisms that live in them. [36] Furthermore, acid rain that lands in a river, or that falls onto land that drains into a river, would make the river more acidic, thereby killing some of the fish and algae in the river. Animal [37] populations, that feed on those aquatic organisms would then suffer as a result.

34

Which choice most logically reflects the writer's reasoning at this point in the passage?

A) NO CHANGE

B) the most robust animal species have adapted to such problematic conditions over time.

C) policies that protect the environment generally curtail industry.

D) neutral rain is generally not detrimental to the health of ecosystems.

35

A) NO CHANGE

B) acidically increasing

C) increasingly acidic

D) increasing or acidic

36

A) NO CHANGE

B) For example,

C) Ironically,

D) Conversely,

37

A) NO CHANGE

B) populations that feed on those aquatic organisms,

C) populations that feed, on those aquatic organisms,

D) populations that feed on those aquatic organisms

CONTINUE

A commonly held belief, and a seemingly obvious one, is that diesel produces more pollutants than refined (petrol) gasoline does. Anyone who has been stuck behind a truck or a bus on the road 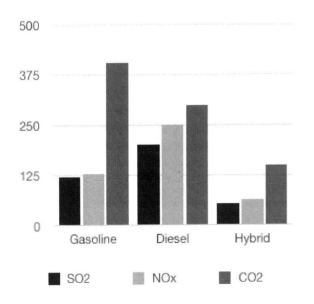38 is seeing the large plumes of grey smog being emitted from those vehicles. Compare that to the almost invisible emissions of a gasoline-powered car. Not surprisingly, 39 gasoline-powered cars emit more SO_2 and NO_x than diesel-powered cars do.

38

A) NO CHANGE
B) will have seen
C) has seen
D) were to see

39

The writer wishes to include an accurate interpretation of the data in the chart. Which choice accomplishes this goal?

A) NO CHANGE
B) gasoline-powered cars emit less SO_2 and NO_x than diesel-powered cars do.
C) gasoline-powered cars emit a larger total mass of pollutants than diesel-powered cars do.
D) gasoline-powered cars emit a smaller total mass of pollutants than diesel-powered cars do.

Selected Emissions for Three Vehicle Types (In Grams Emitted per One Mile Driven)

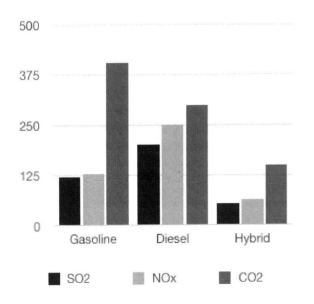

CONTINUE

Still, the choice of an optimal vehicle is not so simple. **40** What about other factors intrinsic to the vehicle itself, such as the weight and the aerodynamic properties of the vehicle's body? Diesel-powered vehicles triumph in respects such as these and also employ a relatively efficient fuel. In addition, a recent study **41** found which modern diesel cars are, surprisingly, **42** with regard to carbonaceous particulate matter now cleaner than gasoline-powered cars (solid particles or liquid droplets that contain carbon).

40

Which question raises an issue that is most clearly relevant to the writer's broader discussion?

A) NO CHANGE

B) What about reduction of other pollutants, such as carbon monoxide, carbon dioxide, and hydrocarbons?

C) What about considerations that would appeal to consumers at the most basic level, such as a vehicle's cost and longevity?

D) What about the cumulative negative effect that even manufacturing the car can have on the ecosystem near a factory?

41

A) NO CHANGE

B) found where

C) found what

D) found that

42

A) NO CHANGE

B) with regard to carbonaceous particulate matter now cleaner than cars powered by gasoline

C) now cleaner than gasoline-powered cars with regard to carbonaceous particulate matter

D) now cleaner than gasoline-powered cars with carbonaceous particulate matter in this regard

CONTINUE

How could this be the case? North American and European diesel cars manufactured in recent years are required to have diesel particle filters, which [43] hurl off the amount of pollutants emitted by those cars. In fact, when researchers sampled cars in six North American and European countries, they found that gas-powered cars emitted 10 times more carbonaceous particulate matter at 22°C and 62 times more at -7°C than diesel cars did.

So, which type of fuel is better for the environment? That question doesn't have a clear answer, and many consumers are looking for alternatives in any case. Because both gasoline and diesel emit harmful compounds, "clean energy" modes of transport, such as electric vehicles and bicycles, are becoming more [44] popular. Interested consumers include those eager to reduce their negative impact on the environment.

43

A) NO CHANGE
B) knock down to nothing
C) hugely obliterate
D) greatly diminish

44

Which choice best combines the sentences at the underlined portion?

A) popular among those eager to reduce
B) popular despite eagerness to reduce
C) popular, and consumers are eager to reduce
D) popular, having with consumers an eagerness to reduce

STOP

**If you finish before time is called, you may check your work on this section only.
Do not turn to any other section.**

Answer Key: Test 8

Passage 1		Passage 2		Passage 3		Passage 4	
1.	B	12.	C	23.	A	34.	D
2.	D	13.	C	24.	A	35.	C
3.	B	14.	D	25.	C	36.	B
4.	C	15.	B	26.	B	37.	D
5.	A	16.	D	27.	B	38.	C
6.	D	17.	C	28.	C	39.	B
7.	A	18.	C	29.	B	40.	B
8.	B	19.	D	30.	C	41.	D
9.	D	20.	A	31.	B	42.	C
10.	D	21.	D	32.	B	43.	D
11.	C	22.	B	33.	C	44.	A

Topic Areas by Question

Expression of Ideas

Passage 1: Questions 2, 5-8, 10

Passage 2: Questions 12, 17-20, 22

Passage 3, Questions 23-24, 26, 28-29, 33

Passage 4, Questions 34, 36, 39-40, 43-44

Standard English Conventions

Passage 1: Questions 1, 3-4, 9, 11

Passage 2: Questions 13-16, 21

Passage 3, Questions 25, 27, 30-32

Passage 4, Questions 35, 37-38, 41-42

Answer Explanations
Test 8, Pages 188-203

Passage 1, Pages 188-191

1. <u>B</u> is the correct answer.

Just as "neither" and "nor" constitute a word pair, "between" and "and" automatically form a pair ("between __ and __") in any sentence in which they are used to coordinate two items. Thus, B is correct, while A, C, and D involve departures from standard English usage.

2. <u>D</u> is the correct answer.

This is a word choice question. The sentence is saying that the river exhibits a unique array of conditions. Thus, D is right. C means the same thing but is too informal. Nothing in the paragraph is about things matching, so A and B are wrong.

3. <u>B</u> is the correct answer.

In this punctuation question, the phrase that starts with "polychlorinated" is a restatement of "toxins," so a comma or dash is appropriate. Thus, B is right. A is wrong because it adds unnecessary words, C has a semicolon, which requires an independent clause on each side of the semicolon (which isn't the case here), and D omits the punctuation altogether.

4. <u>C</u> is the correct answer.

This is a parallelism question. The substances range from "takING on" to another item, so that we need another -ing verb. Thus, C is right. The other choices don't follow the -ing pattern and thus automatically break parallelism.

5. <u>A</u> is the correct answer.

The goal here is to support the idea that the toxins can be traced to General Electric, which is not part of the natural world and could logically manufacture PCBs through non-natural methods. A is the only choice that accomplishes this goal. B (removal), C (harm), and D (the study of PCBs) all raise issues that are not directly related to the question of where PCBs originate.

6. <u>D</u> is the correct answer.

The goal for this question is to support the writer's discussion in this paragraph, which is about PCBs only. Thus, we need an answer choice that is about PCBs. C and D are the only choices that mention PCBs, so rule out A and B. C is also about other toxins, so choose D.

7. <u>A</u> is the correct answer.

A is the only choice that isn't redundant. "Mixed" and "combined" in B are redundant, "left" and "settled" in C are redundant, and "deposited" and "left" in D are redundant.

8. <u>B</u> is the correct answer.

The subject is PCBs, so starting a sentence with "they" makes sense. B is right because it is the only correctly phrased option. A is vague in that is doesn't specify which important people, while the wording in C (indicating a place) and D (describing a substance as an event) doesn't make sense.

9. <u>D</u> is the correct answer.

The only correct phrasing to use with "classified" is "classified as" for something that has been classified. Thus, D is correct. It is easiest to realize this if you read the sentence without the intervening prepositional phrase ("by the Environmental Protection Agency (EPA)").

10. <u>D</u> is the correct answer.

The indented sentence is redundant with information from the previous paragraph ("The National Institute for Occupational Safety and Healthy identified them as a potential carcinogen in the workplace, and the National Toxicology Program has reported that they are likely to cause cancer."). Thus, D is right. Don't be tricked by B; that information isn't the writer's thesis.

11. <u>C</u> is the correct answer.

The subject is "dumping," which is singular. C is correct because it uses a present tense singular verb, while D is wrong because it uses the plural form. A is wrong because the detrimental effects of dumping PCBs have already been established, so the future tense would not make sense here. B creates a sentence fragment (since the main verb in a sentence should not be the -ing form).

Passage 2, Pages 192-195

12. C is the correct answer.

The goal is to introduce the paragraph, which starts with a discussion of tango's image in popular culture. Thus, C is the best option because it leads into the next sentence in the paragraph. B and D are off-topic, while A focuses on tango's influence on film, which is a secondary topic at best.

13. C is the correct answer.

This is a parallelism question. The rest of the paragraph is directed at YOU, so C ("you") matches. A can only function as a plural third-person pronoun, while B and D (though commonly singular, like "you") continue to break the required parallel reference.

14. D is the correct answer.

When answer choices are subsets of each other, check for wordiness. Choices A, B, and C all add unnecessary words. D is the most concise option.

15. B is the correct answer.

The subject is performances, which is plural. Thus, the correct pronoun to use is "they" (choice B). A and D lead to sentence fragments, while C uses incorrect wording that involves at least one ambiguous pronoun in the phrase "those of them."

16. D is the correct answer.

D is right because the conditional ("would/could/should") follows the subjunctive ("if"): "IF you had had the privilege of watching a showcase by Missé and Centurión, you WOULD have witnessed . . . " Choices A, B, and C aren't subjunctive as required by the standard sentence structure.

17. C is the correct answer.

Sentence 1 describes the how "you" would make your way to the dance studio, while sentence 5 continues this topic (and the "you" reference) by describing a possible showcase that the studio hosted. Choose C to effectively group these topics. The placement in A splits the "you" references and prevents the discussion of "artistry" in the previous paragraph from directly transitioning into the discussion of Missé and Centurión, and B also splits the "you" references and makes the reference to "these performances" in sentence 3 unclear. D reverses chronological order, since the description of "you" reaching the studio should come before the description of what "you" would then see there.

18. <u>C</u> is the correct answer.

This paragraph sets up a CONTRAST between "fast movement" and "toned-down." Thus, C is right. The other choices indicate sentence relationships other than contrast: A and D both indicate a sense of clear agreement or concordance, while B indicates that the details presented by the writer should be obvious.

19. <u>D</u> is the correct answer.

The various groups of people were united, or brought together, by tango. Thus, D is right. A is about objects physically sticking together, while B and C don't mean "brought together."

20. <u>A</u> is the correct answer.

Choice A matches the neutral style of the passage. B and C are too informal, while D uses awkward and elevated diction that does not fit the passage. "Scrupulously" often means "honestly" or "ethically," and thus also suggests an improper context for simply not deciding to perform.

21. <u>D</u> is the correct answer.

A comma is needed to separate an introductory phrase (which ends with "the other") from the independent clause. However, no commas are needed in the middle of the introductory phrase in this sentence. Thus, D is right. A, B, and C have extra commas.

22. <u>B</u> is the correct answer.

The goal is to support the idea that Missé and Centurión are "a treat" to watch. Thus, B ("supremely entertaining") is right. This choice also leads well into the next sentence about playfulness. A, C and D are off-topic.

Passage 3, Pages 196-199

23. <u>A</u> is the correct answer.

The phrase "and which contemporary geomatics has adapted to 21st-century technology" is redundant because the paragraph already makes clear that geomatics grew out of land surveying. Thus, A is right, and the fact that the information is clearly presented elsewhere prevents such information from being confusing. Eliminate B, then eliminate C because the writer mostly considers geomatics as a career as the passage progresses, and D because the redundant content does not in any way explain "ancient times."

24. A is the correct answer.

The rise of geomatics was CONCURRENT WITH (time relationship) advancements in technology. Thus, we need a word that means "concurrent with." A is the only choice that fits this context. B indicates a process of working together, C indicates equality or equivalence, and D indicates direction.

25. C is the correct answer.

Commas should not fall in the middle of a unified phrase. Thus, C is right. The structure "combines ___ with ___" does not contain a comma, so eliminate B and D. Similarly, "a discipline that" does not contain a comma, so eliminate A.

26. B is the correct answer.

B is right because it is concise and maintains the third-person style of the passage. The rest of the passage is not addressed to YOU, so eliminate A. C and D are unnecessarily wordy.

27. B is the correct answer.

This sentence defines a term. Thus, it belongs in present tense (choice B). In addition, the verbs in the prior sentence are in present tense and there is no reason to deviate from that pattern.

28. C is the correct answer.

C is right because the sentence is about a cause-and-effect relationship. Data analysis may be useful BECAUSE "geomatics involves being able to understand and analyze geospatial data."

29. B is the correct answer.

The goal here is to offer a relevant supporting detail to projects occurring in the context of INDUSTRY. Thus, B is right. The other three choices are not about industrial applications.

30. C is the correct answer.

The subject of the first part of the sentence is "the activities," while the rest of the sentence is about geomatics. Thus, that new subject needs to be explicitly stated (choose C and eliminate A and B). D switches to the wrong subject (the specialists rather than the field itself).

31. B is the correct answer.

The phrase "including geology, forestry, and fisheries" can be set off with commas or dashes, but not one of each. Because there is one dash at the beginning of that list, another must terminate the list. Thus, B is right.

32. <u>B</u> is the correct answer.

The correct phrase is "may be drawn" (participle), not "may be drew" (incorrect simple past). Furthermore, someone is drawn TO a career. So, after eliminating A and C, eliminate D and choose B.

33. <u>C</u> is the correct answer.

Sentence 5 is about "closely-related" ecological applications. The most RELATED sentence is sentence 3 ("environmental monitoring such as performing environmental impact assessments and pollution control"). Thus, sentence 5 should go right after sentence 3. Sentences 4 and 6 are about software, which is a different field.

Passage 4, Pages 200-203

34. <u>D</u> is the correct answer.

The first paragraph compares harmless neutral rain to harmful acid rain. Thus, D is correct because it reinforces the point that neutral rain isn't harmful. A, B, and C are off-topic (they are about controversy, evolution, and laws, respectively).

35. <u>C</u> is the correct answer.

The word "acidic" is an adjective modifying the noun "rain." Moreover, "increasing" should modify "acidic." Only adverbs (which tend to end in -ly) can modify adjectives, so "increasingly" is the correct form to use. C is the only choice that contains "increasingly" and "acidic."

36. <u>B</u> is the correct answer.

The goal is this question is to figure out the relationship between different phrases: "this acid then damages soil and water systems, as well as the organisms that live in them" and "acid rain that lands in a river, or that falls onto land that drains into a river, would make the river more acidic, thereby killing some of the fish and algae in the river." These ideas agree and the second one is more specific than the first, so choose B and eliminate C and D. Choice A implies that the second sentence makes a different point than the first, which isn't the case here.

37. <u>D</u> is the correct answer.

D is correct because no commas are needed here. A and B are wrong because a subject and verb should not be separated by one comma. (Two commas are used around a phrase if that phrase can be deleted.) C is wrong because "on those aquatic organisms" can not be deleted.

38. <u>C</u> is the correct answer.

This is a verb tense question, so look to other verbs in the sentence to determine the tense. C is right because "HAS been stuck" is parallel (present perfect tense) with "HAS seen." Choice A is present tense, B is future perfect, and D is subjunctive, none of which match present perfect.

39. <u>B</u> is the correct answer.

Based on the graph, gasoline-powered cars emit less SO2 and NOx than diesel-powered cars do. Thus, B is correct. A says the opposite. C and D are outside the scope of the graph, as nothing in the graph is about the total mass of pollutants (only the mass per mile of THREE types of pollutants).

40. <u>B</u> is the correct answer.

The goal here is to provide the most relevant detail, while the discussion itself is about the pollutants emitted by cars. Choice B is the only answer choice about that topic. A is about car design, C is about the considerations of consumers, and trap answer D addresses the damage that could be dealt to ecosystems but does not explicitly mention pollutants in the manner of B.

41. <u>D</u> is the correct answer.

The study found THAT (introducing a statement) modern diesel cars are now cleaner than gasoline-powered cars with regard to carbonaceous particulate matter. Thus, D is right, as "that" properly sets up a fact or a finding. "Which" specifies a subset or an individual item, "where" is for location, and "what" does not make sense in this context.

42. <u>C</u> is the correct answer.

The parenthetical phrase "(solid particles or liquid droplets that contain carbon)" is a definition of carbonaceous particulate matter; thus, "carbonaceous particulate matter" must go immediately before the parenthetical phrase. C is the only choice that features this placement.

43. <u>D</u> is the correct answer.

This is a word choice question, so it is helpful to come up with your own word to substitute for the underlined word. Diesel particle filters REDUCE the amount of pollutants emitted. Thus, we need a word that means "reduce." D ("diminish") is the only choice that fits. A and B are about physically breaking something, while C is awkward and extreme.

44. <u>A</u> is the correct answer.

Clean-energy transport is becoming more popular AMONG eco-conscious consumers. Thus, A is right. B wrongly indicates a contrast, C wrongly indicates a new idea, and D is awkward and wordy.

Made in the USA
Columbia, SC
26 July 2021

42481515R00120